Practical UX Design

A foundational yet practical approach to UX
that delivers more creative, collaborative, holistic,
and mature design solutions, regardless of your
background or experience

Scott Faranello

[PACKT] open source*
community experience distilled
PUBLISHING

BIRMINGHAM - MUMBAI

Practical UX Design

First published: April 2016

Production reference: 1220416

Published by Packt Publishing Ltd.
Livery Place
35 Livery Street
Birmingham B3 2PB, UK.

ISBN 978-1-78588-089-6

www.packtpub.com

Credits

Author
Scott Faranello

Reviewer
Peter Spannagle

Commissioning Editor
Dipika Gaonkar

Acquisition Editor
Subho Gupta

Content Development Editor
Arshiya Ayaz Umer

Technical Editor
Pranjali Mistry

Copy Editor
Karuna Narayanan

Project Coordinator
Kinjal Bari

Proofreader
Safis Editing

Indexer
Rekha Nair

Graphics
Kirk D'Penha

Production Coordinator
Melwyn Dsa

Cover Work
Melwyn Dsa

About the Author

Scott Faranello has been a dedicated and passionate UX professional for well more than a decade now, working with many companies in very diverse organizational cultures. His experience includes intensive customer, user, and business research, conceptual wireframes, designing information architecture, conducting user and usability tests, measuring the ROI of usability, creating visual design, and staying abreast of the current UX technology trends. Scott is also the author of *Balsamiq Wireframes Quickstart Guide (2012)* and *Practical UX Design (2016), Packt Publishing*.

I absolutely could not have written this book without the love, support, and encouragement of my wife Melanie, who got me unstuck when I needed it and who reminded me that the chapters were good enough, or else I'd still be writing Chapter 1. I want to acknowledge my two beautiful boys, who in the past year never saw dad without the laptop—you both are the reason I've accomplished anything at all. I'd also like to thank the fine folks at Packt Publishing, including Subho Gupta, Pranjali Mistry, and of course, Arshiya Ayaz Umer, whose patience never ran out, even when it should have. Thank you for giving me the opportunity to write for you once again and for believing and trusting in me throughout. I'd like to thank my friend Jennifer Fabrizi, who was kind enough to read some of my work when it was still in the larval stage. Thanks to Rob Edge for giving me a much-needed break from thinking about UX one night a week. Thanks to James Wachira because how could I not thank you? Thanks to Greg Renoff, the author of *Van Halen Rising*, who was kind enough to thank me in his book, so I am returning the favor. Thank to Starbucks, Whole Foods, and Panera Bread for allowing me to sit for hours, even during lunch time, as I wrote and rewrote these chapters while consuming most of their coffee. Lastly, I'd like to thank you for buying this book and for taking the time to read what has been the top priority of my life for the past year.

I am grateful. Thank you.

About the Reviewer

Peter Spannagle is a UX design leader and strategist who lives in San Francisco. His background includes working with mobile, agency, start-ups and enterprise. He helps companies define and launch digital products by working with business stakeholders to establish objectives, engaging with end users to capture insights and user needs, leading rounds of concept design and validation, directing creative and technical teams to execute a design vision using iterative and collaborative methods. He is the coauthor of *WordPress and Flash 10.x Cookbook*, Packt Publishing, 2010.

www.PacktPub.com

eBooks, discount offers, and more

Did you know that Packt offers eBook versions of every book published, with PDF and ePub files available? You can upgrade to the eBook version at `www.PacktPub.com` and as a print book customer, you are entitled to a discount on the eBook copy. Get in touch with us at `customercare@packtpub.com` for more details.

At `www.PacktPub.com`, you can also read a collection of free technical articles, sign up for a range of free newsletters and receive exclusive discounts and offers on Packt books and eBooks.

`https://www2.packtpub.com/books/subscription/packtlib`

Do you need instant solutions to your IT questions? PacktLib is Packt's online digital book library. Here, you can search, access, and read Packt's entire library of books.

Why subscribe?

- Fully searchable across every book published by Packt
- Copy and paste, print, and bookmark content
- On demand and accessible via a web browser

To Mel and the boys. My miracles.

Table of Contents

Preface

"If you have built castles in the air, your work need not be lost; that is where they should be. Now put the foundations under them."

– Henry David Thoreau

It's an exciting time for User Experience (UX). Never before has UX been so much at the forefront of technology and so sought after by companies around the world. It's truly a great time to be a UX practitioner. It has also taken a long time to reach this place. UX has been working hard for years to make an impact on becoming an integral and valued member of the technology team, proving its value and providing organizations with problem-solving techniques and design solutions that promise greater returns on investment (ROI) and happier customers and users. Nevertheless, while UX appears to be highly sought after, garnering high salaries in many areas and seemingly plentiful job opportunities appearing almost daily, there is another story taking place that is not as rosy.

Although UX is more prevalent in business circles, it is still highly misunderstood. A gap exists between how UX sees itself and what stakeholders and executive understand of it. To those at the top as well as managers, stakeholders, project managers, and so on, UX practitioners are thought of as those folks who perform usability studies and wireframes, usually after business requirements have been completed and the development team is about to launch a product. The rest of the time, UX teams can sit idle, waiting to be asked on a project while watching user-facing products continue being released for the public without their help.

Even as calls to customer support increase as revenue from poor design decisions goes down, UX still has trouble proving its value. With the current pace of technology and the competitive nature of interactive designs, it is more important than ever for companies to keep pace and meet the expectations of their customers/users. UX is much more than usability studies and wireframes.

UX is a mindset that requires a deep understanding, strategy, and approach toward design that when aligned to business goals has the potential to go straight to the top, grabbing the attention of those who matter most: those who pay us to deliver results. When the opportunity of writing this book came to me, I was, of course, very excited and also quite challenged. While it's important to share the techniques and skills that UX practitioners need in order to improve their design work, it was also important to focus on UX from a more holistic perspective to understand and explain how it is connected and related to the larger world of design, creativity, and the human experience.

To accomplish this in a book, I provided material that speaks not only to new UX practitioners, but also to anyone at any level, be they technology or business-focused learners and those in the UX field those who want to understand what UX is, what UX does, and how UX can truly provide real, measurable business value business stakeholders find impossible to ignore. You will also find no geekspeak in these pages. Anytime a technical term is introduced, a clear explanation follows. UX is about reaching large audiences with design, and writing about it should be no different. In addition, when we talk only to those in the UX field, we do our profession and ourselves a disservice. UX is about access, ease of use, and engagement. Unless our coworkers understand UX clearly, we cannot expect to deliver clarity to our end users. This is what *Practical UX* sets out to accomplish.

UX is not going away anytime soon, but if we fail to engage, educate, and prove our value on a consistent and visible basis to our entire audience—customers, users, and business stakeholders—we risk losing our audience for good. Good UX design is more than just look and feel and the most effective place on the screen to put a submit button. Those things are important, but good UX is more importantly about the mindset, creativity, and recognizing that our true value lies in how we think and how we approach our work. We will begin with the mindset of UX and what it means to truly listen to customers/users. We will then move on to creativity and how to identify a truly good design using examples from the Web, mobile, and areas of design that at first may seem far outside the realm of UX, but upon closer inspection are actually inseparable from it. Following that, we will look at how to effectively drive customers, users, and stakeholders to where we want them to go in terms of information architecture, pattern usage, and a strategy that provides stakeholders and business leaders with results that are impossible to ignore. Lastly, we will look at some of the tools of the UX trade as well as resources to expand your learning long after our time together here.

Practical UX is a big subject that will take you down many interesting and hopefully new paths of learning in order to take your design skills and UX knowledge to the highest level of maturity.

Thank you for taking this journey with me. Now, let's begin.

What this book covers

Chapter 1, The User Experience Mindset, looks at some persistent myths about design and customer/user engagement that can make a profession like UX non-existent. Dispelling these myths is the first step, and an important one, for acquiring a UX mindset—the first step of good design.

Chapter 2, Creative UX, looks at how to create six optimal conditions for your best ideas to appear. This will require two modes of thinking, open and closed. Once you acquire the skill to control both of these mindsets creativity and good design will soon follow.

Chapter 3, Good UX Design, identifies ten design principles found in all good UX design, how to identify it and how to recognize it is more than just web design. Good design has no boundaries and this chapter will explain why.

Chapter 4, Foundations of Good IA, will provide you with a broader understanding of Information Architecture (IA) that will give you a wider view of IA and demonstrate that IA is not found in technology.

Chapter 5, Patterns, Properties, and Principles of a Good UX Design, looks at some fundamental properties of patterns that are found is all of the best designs, from UX to music to painting to architecture. Borrowing from a renowned building architect, you will be introduced to fifteen properties that will change the way you look and think about patterns and how to use them in your design work.

Chapter 6, An Essential Strategy for UX Maturity, discusses the challenges that UX faces if its maturity level does not increase. Doing this effectively and rapidly begins with a strategy that transforms how others, like stakeholders and various other colleagues, understand the true value of UX work.

Chapter 7, UX Tools, hows you the most important tools of the UX trade that never go out of style.

Chapter 8, Final Thoughts and Additional Resources, provides resources for continued learning long after you have finished reading this book.

What you need for this book

No software is needed for this book.

Who this book is for

This book is intended for UX practitioner/designers and anyone who is engaged in designing UX for end users, where you are looking to go deep and become fully engaged with your surroundings, team, end users, and your organization. This is also a book for those who are not yet enlightened about the value of UX, those curious about those who may be curious have never taken the time to investigate what UX is all about, this book is also for teachers of UX, IT, and other disciplines where customers and end users are important. The bottom line is that regardless of who you are or where you come from, this book provides a rich, in-depth, and insightful approach to UX that will help you to become a better UX designer, practitioner, thinker and leader.

Conventions

In this book, you will find a number of text styles that distinguish between different kinds of information. Here are some examples of these styles and an explanation of their meaning.

New terms and **important words** are shown in bold. Words that you see on the screen, for example, in menus or dialog boxes, appear in the text like this: "To clarify the issue even further, Apple added a line of text below the app name that says, **Offers in-App Purchases** to avoid unnecessary and annoying surprises later."

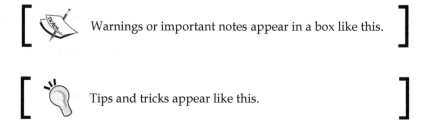

Warnings or important notes appear in a box like this.

Tips and tricks appear like this.

Reader feedback

Feedback from our readers is always welcome. Let us know what you think about this book—what you liked or disliked. Reader feedback is important for us as it helps us develop titles that you will really get the most out of.

To send us general feedback, simply e-mail feedback@packtpub.com, and mention the book's title in the subject of your message.

If there is a topic that you have expertise in and you are interested in either writing or contributing to a book, see our author guide at www.packtpub.com/authors.

Customer support

Now that you are the proud owner of a Packt book, we have a number of things to help you to get the most from your purchase.

Downloading the color images of this book

We also provide you with a PDF file that has color images of the screenshots/ diagrams used in this book. The color images will help you better understand the changes in the output. You can download this file from `http://www.packtpub.com/ sites/default/files/downloads/PracticalUXDesign_ColorImages.pdf`.

Errata

Although we have taken every care to ensure the accuracy of our content, mistakes do happen. If you find a mistake in one of our books — maybe a mistake in the text or the code — we would be grateful if you could report this to us. By doing so, you can save other readers from frustration and help us improve subsequent versions of this book. If you find any errata, please report them by visiting `http://www.packtpub. com/submit-errata`, selecting your book, clicking on the **Errata Submission Form** link, and entering the details of your errata. Once your errata are verified, your submission will be accepted and the errata will be uploaded to our website or added to any list of existing errata under the Errata section of that title.

To view the previously submitted errata, go to `https://www.packtpub.com/books/ content/support` and enter the name of the book in the search field. The required information will appear under the **Errata** section.

Piracy

Piracy of copyrighted material on the Internet is an ongoing problem across all media. At Packt, we take the protection of our copyright and licenses very seriously. If you come across any illegal copies of our works in any form on the Internet, please provide us with the location address or website name immediately so that we can pursue a remedy.

Please contact us at `copyright@packtpub.com` with a link to the suspected pirated material.

We appreciate your help in protecting our authors and our ability to bring you valuable content.

Questions

If you have a problem with any aspect of this book, you can contact us at questions@packtpub.com, and we will do our best to address the problem.

1

The User Experience Mindset

"Silicon Valley is a mindset, not a location."

– Reid Hoffman

Let's begin by introducing the first topic that every **User Experience** (**UX**) practitioner, and business stakeholder needs to understand about UX: The mindset of UX and what it means to think like a UX practitioner. However, before we do that, let's understand something about UX itself.

UX is a skill. It's a practice. It's about where to place a button on a website and how to organize content. It's about how to improve screen and interface design. It's about wireframes, focus groups, and usability studies. These are the things we know about UX, but what else should we know?

UX is also about collaboration. It's about solving problems and finding solutions. UX is about looking at the world with a unique perspective and a unique mindset. UX is also about focusing on the right people at the right time, including customers, end users and also stakeholders whose business goals and objectives are directly related to UX decisions. As you will see, however, UX is harder to get across than you might think. Good design may seem like a no brainer, but, it is not that simple.

In this chapter we will look at:

- The myths about mindset
- Solving problems effectively
- Examples of using the UX mindset
- The perils of ignoring UX

Let's begin with a story, a myth if you will, that needs to be dispelled if we expect to deliver better design though UX, better solutions and help those who need our help to understand our true value.

Dispelling the myth of "faster horses"

"If I had asked people what they wanted, they would have said faster horses."

– Henry Ford

If you've been in the corporate world or in technology for any length of time, you have probably heard this quote. It implies, albeit subtly, that engaging users in order to find out what they need or want is not important because, hey, what do they know? Seeing this quote and hearing it used for so long, it always seemed odd that Ford would say such a thing. It was also compelling to find out whether he actually did. Not surprisingly, when you do a little digging, you find rather quickly that something is amiss.

The "faster horses" quote is actually relatively new, first appearing around the year 2001 in a letter sent to the UK publication *Marketing Week*. Additional research by the Henry Ford Museum found that this quote never appeared in any of Ford's own letters and writings. The museum also claimed that while "Mr. Ford wrote numerous articles for a variety of periodicals and newspapers, the quotes attributed to him were varied and often unsubstantiated." – https://www.quora.com/. Hmmm...so if Ford never said it, why does it persist and why is it attributed to a man who was highly innovative, creative, and effective in the solutions he delivered on a global scale?

This quote originated in a marketing publication. The differences between marketing and UX have always been quite diverse. Marketing tends to view customers from an inside-out perspective evidenced by its strong focus on new customer acquisition and customer retention. UX views its customers from the outside in, working closely with them to understand the problems they face and helping to solve them.

Viewed with a marketing mindset, "faster horses" implies that a designer or an inventor, in the case of Henry Ford, knew better than his customers. Looking from the inside-out, "faster horses" implies that we can make assumptions about our customers/users based on data, usage patterns and thinking that if we did ask customers they would not really know what was best for them. The "faster horses" quote also implies that designers can impact a customer's experience based solely on intuition, instincts, experience and business smarts instead of in-depth research and engagement. The "faster horses" quote does one more thing as well: it makes the role of a UX practitioner much harder.

For starters, "faster horses" thinking diminishes the understanding of what UX does and how its solutions rely on understanding customers and end users. It also undercuts the ability of UX practitioners to engage in customer/user facing projects because those with the "faster horses" mindset can just do it themselves and then just pass along their work to the UX folks to test it for any last minute usability and interaction issues. Is it the best solution? Maybe or maybe not, but so long as end users can do the tasks then that is good enough.

"Faster horses" thinking also discounts the level of research and trial and error required to deliver real solutions, not just for customers but for business success as well. As we will see in later chapter, there is much more to problem solving than assuming we know what customers want. "Faster horses" thinking also implies that great design can be done in a vacuum, where anyone with enough experience can design and deliver a customer-/user-based solution without having to engage users face to face. "Faster horses" thinking also allows designers to avoid the discomfort sometimes associated with creativity; something we will look at in the next chapter. The reality is that ignoring our customers/users and thinking we know best can cause many problems, like project failures, over spending, underperforming and lowering user efficiency, effectiveness and satisfaction. These can have huge implications and unless the mindset of "faster horses" is changed these problems will continue to grow. While going it alone may paint a romantic image of a lone inventor or experienced team delivering what the world needs and making history doing it, realistically it is impossible to do without deep research, customer/user engagement and empathy for the user and stakeholders as well whose goal it is improve business outcomes in a consistently provable and measurable way. The only true approach, therefore, is one that utilizes a truly authentic UX mindset.

The disservice of "faster horses"

Romanticizing lone wolves: people who seemingly go it alone and solve major problems without the help of others, provides us with great stories and legends, but it also does a disservice to the hard work, skill, collaboration, trial and error, problem-solving skills, and the mindset necessary to make it all happen.

There is actually a lot of evidence to support this. It is most readily seen with the amount of projects that fail every year due to teams inadequately addressing customer/user needs. For example, in a video presentation by Dr. Susan Weinschenk of Human Factors International, titled *The ROI of User Experience*, Dr. Weinschenk stated that the amount of money spent worldwide on projects related to **Information Technology (IT)** is estimated at $1 trillion per year. The number of projects abandoned because they are hopelessly inadequate is 15 percent. Refer to http://www.humanfactors.com/project/index.asp for more information on human factors and its importance in project success.

This means $150 billion is wasted each year because teams are not utilizing the right mindset when it matters most, that is, before projects go into development; before requirements are defined; after adequate communication with customers, end users, developers and stakeholders has occurred; and that everyone is in agreement. Dr. Weinschenk also pointed out the problem of office politics, where teams often branch off into silos of ownership. Then, when projects fail to deliver blame is placed elsewhere, further dividing teams that should be working together towards a single, company/business focused goal. Dr. Weinschenk further pointed out that in order to solve this problem, teams need to get out in front of these issues using techniques such as business and user research and data and analytics to determine business and customer related metrics, interviewing **subject matter experts (SMEs)** , customers and users, usability testing, root-cause analysis, prototyping and wireframing. All these techniques play a major role in establishing a UX mindset because we are no longer thinking as separate teams. We are now thinking as a unit with the right focus on effective outcomes and measurable results.

When facts ruin a good story

Let's pretend for a moment that Henry Ford actually did utter those words about "faster horses." How would this story hold up when we look at the reality of the situation? Were people in 1908 really looking for faster horses? Were they truly oblivious to the real problems that horse-powered transportation created by the turn of the century? Also, if people *were* really interested in faster horses, where were they going in such a hurry? Doing some research on the subject, one quickly discovers that the truth is often much more interesting and also much different than what we are led to believe.

By 1908, there were hundreds of thousand of horses crowding city streets around the world, and this was not a new problem. In fact, the problems with horses were well-known. For example, by 1894:

> *"London…had 11,000 cabs, all horse-powered…several thousand buses, each of which required 12 horses per day, a total of more than 50,000 horses. In addition, there were countless carts, drays, and wains, all working constantly to deliver the goods needed by the rapidly growing population of what was then the largest city in the world. Similar figures could be produced for any great city of the time."*
>
> – Stephen Davies, The Great Horse-Manure Crisis of 1894

One can only imagine the impact this had on crowded streets, not to mention the smell. Getting around must have been quite difficult. Getting anywhere faster in the conditions would be better served with flying horses rather than faster ones. In addition, the majority of the population in 1908 were living in cities, most within walking distance of their jobs. Trains and subways existed too too, as did automobiles. Automobiles were only more of a luxury item that the working class could not afford.

In light of all of this evidence, there is no mention of faster horses, not does it sound like anyone would have been asking for one. Now, if this isn't enough evidence, horses in 1908 were also quite dangerous. In fact, by 1916, there were 16.9 horse-related fatalities per 10,000 horse-drawn vehicles, a number said to be seven times that of Chicago's automobile fatality rate in 1997!

> *"The skittishness of horses added a dangerous level of unpredictability to nineteenth-century transportation. This was particularly true in a bustling urban environment, full of surprises that could shock and spook the animals. Horses often stampeded, but a more common danger came from horses kicking, biting, or trampling bystanders. Children were particularly at risk."*
>
> *–Eric Morris, From Horse Power to Horsepower*

Don't forget the mortality rate of horses (Warning: This is not for the squeamish).

City dwelling horses often fell on average of once every hundred miles of travel. If the horse (weighing an average of 1,300 pounds), was badly injured it would be shot on the spot and left to die, creating a ghastly obstruction that clogged streets and brought traffic to a halt. Special horse-removal services did exist at the time, but moving such a large carcass was not easy. As a result, street cleaners often waited for the corpses to putrefy so the dead horse could be sawed into pieces and carted off.

Problem solved? Well, there was also the problem of the smell, the flies, the horribleness of dead horses on the street and of course the risk of disease — *Eric Morris, From Horse Power to Horsepower.*

Source: http://i.imgur.com/U6ZC3ki.jpg

Now, with these conditions in mind, place yourself in 1908 as an inventor/ businessman like Henry Ford. As you are researching on these problems and seeing them firsthand, would you be so callous and indifferent to these problems? Does it make sense in light of this history that Henry Ford would have ignored what people were experiencing, himself included, and think they were ignorant enough to simply want faster horses? Of course, not. These problems were impossible to ignore.

In fact, 10 years before Ford's Model-T arrived on the scene, the first ever city-planning meeting convened in New York City to address the problems facing large cities. One major concern was also related to horses, namely the overwhelming amount of horse manure infesting city streets. One reporter wrote in the *Times of London* that 50 years hence, every street in London would be buried under nine feet of manure. — *The Great Horse-Manure Crisis of 1894, Stephen Davies.*

Faster horses? Hardly. To solve these major problems would require far more than just guesswork and assumptions. It would require research, ethnography, concept design, trial and error, testing, and so on.

So, what did Ford do in light of these problems? Did he invent the world's largest pooper-scooper, a more efficient way to kill the millions of flies born out of the tons of manure and dead horses? Did he strap rockets on the backs of horses to get them airborne or give everyone oxygen masks to simply deal with the problem? Of course not. He did something much smarter. No, he didn't invent the automobile. That was done a decade earlier by Gottlieb Daimler and Karl Benz, inventors of the high-speed gasoline engine in the 1880s— *The Origins*, `mercedes-benz.com.au`

Source: `http://gottliebdaimler.blogspot.com/`

Instead, Ford saw the problems that horses created, the conditions people were living in and the salaries people were making—on average, the living wage in 1908 was 22 cents per hour with the average worker bringing home between $200 and $400 per year—and delivered a solution that solved all of these problems at once. His solution was to invent the world's first assembly line where his inexpensive Model-T automobile could be made cheaply, quickly, and in large numbers. By 1914, just six years after introducing the Model-T, it sold more than *all other automakers combined.—Ford Model T, Wikipedia, the free encyclopedia.* Quite an accomplishment for someone who supposedly ignored his customers and thought all they really wanted were faster horses.

Regardless of the facts, the "faster horses" myth still persists. It is troubling to consider, but it could very well be a convenient way to rationalize avoiding customer engagement due to the time and money required to do it effectively. It may also be a response to a culture where siloed teams can continue to place blame when things go wrong.

> *"When problems arise..." the enemy" becomes the players at the other positions, or even the customers...precluding any opportunity to learn from each others' experience."*
>
> *–Peter Senge, The Fifth Discipline.*

Collaboration is a joke, but nobody is laughing

Consider the following illustration. You may be familiar with it. It's popular with project designers and developers and often found on cubicle walls as an amusing depiction of how technology teams interpret the needs of their customers/users:

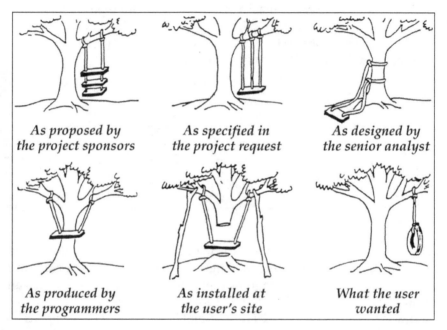

Source: http://www.businessballs.com/images/treeswing/tree-swing-s-hogh.jpg

The preceding image is amusing because if you work in the world of technology and solution delivery it is something you experience on a regular basis. It is also a stark reminder of what happens when we allow a "faster horses" approach to problem solving. Instead of working through the problems as a collaborative team where diverse skills such as UX should be included, teams are singularly focused, work in silos, develop solutions based on their specific understanding of the problem and are often guided to those conclusions by inadequate business/customer/user requirements that lack the input of a unified, cross-disciplined, cross-collaborative team. In addition, any customer/user solution hypothesis goes untested while business/customer/user related research, if any is done at all, scratches the surface or is so disjointed and disconnected that nothing can get accomplished to truly serve the end user's needs. As we can see in the preceding illustration, when projects fail as a result, it is far easier to place blame elsewhere while continuing to overlook the real problems at hand.

In light of the preceding illustration, some questions come to mind, ones you might want to try and answer. Here are some of them:

- Are teams spending too little time researching and engaging with their customers and users, and instead, rushing to solutions?

- Are teams truly considering the implications of their design decisions or simply subscribing to a *just get it done* mentality, which distracts from diagnosing the real problems?

- What does "speed" to market really mean? Does it mean surpassing the competition in terms of delivering innovation to customers/users or does it mean delivering products quick enough to be able to say, "Look how fast we can deliver something?"

The answers may be that it is far easier, less uncomfortable and less expensive to stay in silos rather than engage with other skill sets such as UX, that they may not clearly understand. In addition, going it alone has a romantic element to it that allows for successful teams to take all the credit and unsuccessful ones to place blame. As UX practitioners, it may be up to us to solve this problem once and for all and demonstrate through example how the UX mindset brings people together to solve real problems in a measurable way and to learn from our failures in order to improve, not for our own benefit, but for the benefit of those who truly need our help.

Understanding the problem

"The problem is we don't understand the problem"

– Paul MacCready

In 1977, Paul MacCready, an American aeronautical engineer, won the Kremer prize, "a monetary award…given to pioneers of human-powered flight." MacCready succeeded where for 20 years design teams were unable to. The challenge was how to design an aircraft that could be powered by human muscle and ingenuity alone, and stay aloft long enough to complete "a figure-eight course covering a total of one mile." Year after year design teams built wonderfully crafted, self-powered machines, but all failed to fly the distance, often crashing and needing a year or more to repair the damage and try again.

Think about this problem for a moment and consider how you might go about solving it. Would you change the design by looking for the faults in the flying mechanisms? Would you find a stronger pilot who could pedal longer or faster? Would you spend more time practicing flying a similar course before attempting to win the prize? Or would you try something entirely different?

MacCready thought about this too, but rather than assume he knew the answer, he spent time observing and researching until the answer became clear. Rather than building a plane that could stay in the air longer, fly further or faster, MacCready realized that all of the other aircrafts attempting to win the prize failed, not because of their design, but because of the time it took to rebuild their aircraft after crashing. As a result MacCready and his team designed an aircraft that could still crash, but if it did it could be rebuilt in a matter of days instead of months or years. In other words, MacCready's design allowed him to fail, learn and try again more often than his competition.

> *"The first airplane didn't work. It was too flimsy. But, because the problem [MacCready] set out to solve was creating a plane he could fix in hours, he was able to quickly iterate…rebuild, retest [and] relearn…from months and years to hours and days."*

> *–Aza Raskin, You Are Solving The Wrong Problem*

Here is an image of MacCready's prize winning aircraft, the Gossamer Albatross:

Source: https://en.wikipedia.org/wiki/MacCready_Gossamer_Albatross

You can read more about MacCready 's Gossamer Albatross at
`https://en.wikipedia.org/wiki/MacCready_Gossamer_Albatross`.

MacCready's approach to research, observation, learning through failure, iterating, and trying again before putting it in front of the judges, which in our case is our customers and users, is what the UX mindset is all about and is our ultimate goal as UX designers and practitioners. Think of MacCready's approach to problem solving the next time you approach a problem. Here is the recipe:

- Deep, customer-/user-engaged research
- Close observation of your end users
- Identify root causes
- Develop a hypothesis based on your research
- Test your hypothesis through prototyping and wireframes
- Fail and try again
- Improve on your failures
- Test again
- Fail again (perhaps)
- Improve, test, fail, and continuing to repeat these steps
- Execute, compete, and win

There are, of course, many details that make up each of these bullets points and we will continue to establish them through the rest of this book, but hopefully, you get the idea. This is a recipe that prioritizes research, problem solving, root-cause analysis, testing, and iterating between ideas and execution while emphasizing failure as essential in order to learn and make it better before presenting it to the judges. It is also a recipe for bringing project teams together to solve problems. Keep in mind, however, that this is not easy to accomplish. The challenge, as you will discover, involves convincing teams to drop "faster horses" thinking and approach problems differently. This is not an easy thing to do, however, when this way of thinking is so engrained in our culture.

Customers/users are dumb!

There's a classic episode of the Simpsons where Homer's long-lost brother asked him to design a new car for the everyday person. Although the design engineers attempted to ignore Homer, his brother forced the issue and the results were utterly predictable:

Source: http://www.geek.com/wp-content/uploads/2015/09/thehomer.jpg

By dropping the company's "faster horse" mentality, Homer's new car was designed with customer/user feedback. The design of course is completely absurd and so predictable, coming from someone as empty headed as Homer. The cartoon also drives home another more subtle point: the customer isn't very bright. In the end, Homer's design failed, followed by the automaker going out of business while his long-lost brother was once again estranged from his brother, this time, we can assume, for good.

Somehow have have convinced ourselves that asking people what they want is a recipe for disaster and that listening to customers will create more disasters like Homer's car and less like what people really need. Therefore, the message is to leave designing to the professionals and not in the hands of people who will actually be using it.

> *"Customers should not be trusted to come up with solutions; they aren't expert or informed enough for that part of the innovation process. That's what your R&D team is for...What form the solutions take should be up to you, and you alone."*
>
> – *Anthony W. Ulwick, Turn Customer Input into Innovation*

Shut up and listen!

To be absolutely clear, as trained UX designers it is ultimately up to us to fill in the holes and interpret what we are hearing and seeing into educated guesses or hypothesis to be tested by our customers and users to see whether we are correct and that we heard them correctly. Listening to our customers and end users is not detrimental to our success, rather it is integral to it, provided we know how to listen and how to interpret what we are hearing and seeing and turning that into viable design solutions. This takes time, effort, and skill. To go the other route and think that we have to either follow what our customers say and fail or ignore them and succeed is risking failure on a large scale. For example, in an article from the Harvard Business Review by Anthony W. Ulwick, titled *Turn Customer Input into Innovation*, the author shared an example of how one company, Kawasaki, learned a valuable lesson in not only listening to customers, but more importantly, paying attention and deciphering what is really needed as a result.

> *"When [Kawasaki] asked users what could be done to improve [their] Jet Ski's ride, customers requested extra padding on the vehicle's sides to make the standing position more comfortable. It never occurred to them to request a seated watercraft. The company focused on giving customers what they asked for, while other manufacturers began to develop seated models that since have bumped Kawasaki — famed for its motorcycles, which are never ridden standing — from its leading market position."*

It seems hard to believe that experienced designers would take comments like these so literally, yet the business and product world is full of similar stories. Engaging with our customers and users is a balance. It is not either…or. It is a relationship and an understanding that requires deep engagement informed by experience, design expertise and a little psychology thrown in as well. It requires a UX mindset in order to see what others cannot and to really understand what our customers and users are telling us. It is then up to us to interpret, test and see whether we were correct. If not, try again quickly until it's right. When we fail to interpret customer/user needs correctly, however, it is easier to place blame on the customer and the end user than to acknowledge that it was our design that failed because we didn't really listen. There is even an acronym for this phenomenon: "PICNIC" or problem in chair, not in computer. — http://www.userfocus.co.uk/articles/picnic.html. Here is a quote that drives this point home quite nicely:

> *"If there is any one secret of success, it lies in the ability to get the other person's point of view and see things from that person's angle as well as from your own."*

> *– Henry Ford*

This is a quote that Henry Ford actually said, verifiably so! — *How to Win Friends & Influence People*, Dale Carnegie.

Data-driven design

One of the things we talked about in this chapter is getting to root causes, which is a key element of the UX mindset. Root causes are found when you pull back all the layers of a problem until you can no longer ask *why* and are ready to ask *how* are you going to solve the problem. This requires asking the right questions that will not only solve customer/user problems, but will solve stakeholder needs as well.

For example, asking stakeholders:

- What is the current business problem?
- How do you know it's a problem?
- What are the measurable business goals and objectives, otherwise known as **key performance indicators (KPIs)**?
- How will we know we are successful?
- What business areas/systems/applications are impacted?
- What are the risks to the company, our customers and our users if we don't solve it?

These are hard questions, but important ones because they challenge stakeholders to think about why we are solving a problem and how to do it. It also gets stakeholders engaged in the process. Without this approach there is no way to know what is broken and by how much. Every problem worth solving must be evidenced based using the current version of a system, if possible, to understand what is in need of repair.

Despite the importance of data and its proven value, many companies still do not track it with regards to translating metrics into good design, something we will talk about in depth in a later chapter. Without knowing what you are trying to measure and what the current baseline to measure against is, you are essentially designing blind; the equivalent of throwing darts hoping to hit the bullseye. The problem is you will be throwing them while blindfolded and at a moving target.

Asking hard question will provide real numbers that you can design against and test to see whether your assumptions are correct. You can then track these numbers later when the product launches to make sure your improvements are effective, from a customer/user and business perspective.

"The process of innovation begins with identifying the outcomes customers want to achieve; it ends in the creation of items they will buy...When desired outcomes become the focus of customer research, innovation is no longer a matter of wish fulfillment or serendipity; it is instead a manageable, predictable discipline."

– Anthony W. Ulwick, Turn Customer Input into Innovation

The meme that just won't die

By now, we've dispelled the "faster horse" myth once and for all. No longer will we utter this quote, nor will we allow others to do so in our presence, without sharing with them why it's short sighted and wrong. We are also in a better position to correct them because we are thinking with a UX mindset that will guide us to better solutions, right? There is, however, one problem. As I stated earlier, Ford's supposed "faster horse" quote is not the only one of its kind.

"We built [the Mac] for ourselves. We were the group of people who were going to judge whether it was great or not. We weren't going to go out and do market research."

– Steve Jobs

Oh no. Here we go again! Let's put a stop to it right now with this: Steve Jobs did not ignore his customers! In fact, Jobs listened intensely to them.

"Really great products come from melding two points of view – the technology point of view and the customer point of view. You need both...It takes a long time to pull out of customers what they really want, and it takes a long time to pull out of technology what it can really give."

– An interview with Steven Jobs, Inc.'s Entrepreneur of the Decade, by Bo Burlingham.

Source: http://stylemagazine.com/news/2015/feb/06/apple-ceo-who-fired-steve-jobs-i-wish-i-had-hired

As we mentioned earlier, listening is key, and interpreting what is said is even more important. To put it another way, don't provide your customers with a more comfortable way of standing when sitting is preferred, and don't provide them with a faster horse when an affordable automobile makes more sense. Good design is not about assuming the truth. Good design is about knowing is the truth based on research, testing and more testing to validate your assumptions and then to compare the data. Only then will you prove that your design truly makes a difference.

Design thinking: an idea worth investing in

When you are ready to start designing solutions based on all the pre-work you've done: understanding your stakeholders/customers/users, the technology available, the long-term return on investment and of course the human aspect, that is, will people like and use what you give them, you will then want to begin working on a solution with a team. Henry Ford and Steve Jobs did not work alone and neither should you. One way to do this is using a technique called **Design Thinking**.

Design thinking originated at The School of Engineering at California's Stanford University with a course designed to prepare *a generation of innovators to tackle complex challenges*. Design thinking challenges participants to solve problems by first defining them and then iterating as a collaborative team focused on developing *an unexpected range of possible solutions…to take back out into the field and test with real people.*—http://dschool.stanford.edu/our-point-of-view/.

Designing thinking follows a very simple approach to problem solving that introduces the UX mindset to those who may not have experienced it before. Here are the steps:

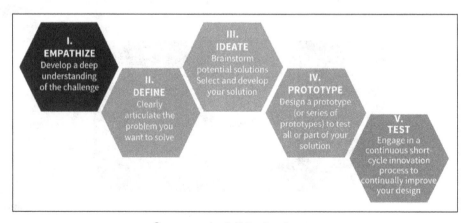

Source: springhillschool.org

We can break this down even further, taking into consideration three of the most important areas of focus: technology, business, and human values, as shown here:

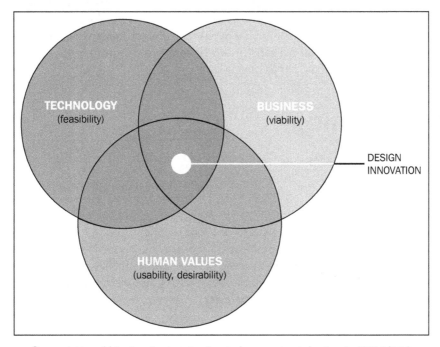

Source: http://dschool.stanford.edu/wp-content/uploads/2010/09/
venn_diagram-730x523.jpg

- **Technology (feasibility)**: This is the "how "of product design. It refers to how we make it happen with what we have at our disposal, such as, technology, budgetary constraints, stakeholder goals, user/customer problems, and so on.

- **Business (viability)**: This refers to long-term return on investment (ROI) and how long it will take to reach those goals.

- **Human values (usability, desirability)**: This refers to the reactions from customers/users. Will people like our solution and use it? Will they be excited about it? Is it unique and easy to use? Does it solve an identifiable problem that we have observed through research and observation?

"You realize that you aren't going to solve the problem sitting in an office, you need to get out and talk to the people who are actually dealing with it, whether that's your customers or your front-line employees."

– Design Thinking graduate.

In 2006, the design thinking program at Standford, also known as d.School, launched a week-long education program for managers and executives called **Customer-Focused Innovation (CFI)**, where participants from across industries approached problems in a collaborative setting and from the customers' point of view. As of this writing, admission to CFI is approx $15,000 for one week of training, teamwork, creativity, and innovation. That's quite an investment and a positive development in dispelling the "faster horses" myth once and for all.

One more thing

"There is nothing in a caterpillar that tells you it's going to be a butterfly."

– Richard Buckminster "Bucky" Fuller

There is a cemetery in Watertown, MA with a grave marker that reads, "Call me trim tab. Bucky." This is the final resting place of Richard Buckminster "Bucky" Fuller, an American architect, author, designer and inventor. He is perhaps best known for developing the structural mathematics of the geodesic dome, an example of which can be seen in the following image, otherwise known as Spaceship Earth from Disney World's Epcot Center theme park.

Source: https://upload.wikimedia.org/wikipedia/commons/7/7a/Spaceship_Earth_2.jpg

Fuller was a problem solver and a big thinker who took on very challenging problems, concepts and ideas with passion and a perspective very reminiscent of the UX mindset.

> *"If you are in a shipwreck and all the boats are gone, a piano top buoyant enough to keep you afloat that comes along makes a fortuitous life preserver. But this is not to say that the best way to design a life preserver is in the form of a piano top. I think that we are clinging to a great many piano tops in accepting yesterday's fortuitous contriving's as constituting the only means for solving a given problem."*

> *– R. Buckminster Fuller*

Fuller understood that solving problems and reaching conclusions meant challenging what we think we know and learning more about what we don't in order that we might find what Fuller referred to as the non-obvious and thus far better solutions:

> *"Everything you've learned in school as obvious becomes less and less obvious as you begin to study the universe. For example, there are no solids in the universe. There's not even a suggestion of a solid. There are no absolute continuums. There are no surfaces. There are no straight lines."*

> *– R. Buckminster Fuller*

To better explain this type of problem solving mindset, Fuller used the metaphor of a "trim tab," a small rudder connected to a larger rudder found on ships and airplanes. Here is an example of a trimtab:

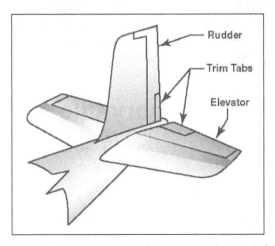

Source: http://d1br7wc30ambms.cloudfront.net/wp-content/uploads/2015/05/trimtabs.jpg

A trim tab is used to turn a very large object with minimal effort, as Wikipedia explains:

> *"The use of trim tabs significantly reduces a pilot's workload during continuous maneuvers…allowing them to focus their attention on other tasks such as traffic avoidance or communication with air traffic control."*

> *– Trim tab, From Wikipedia, the free encyclopedia*

Another reason for Fuller's interest in the trim tab was its small size compared to the larger whole. Based on its relative size compared to the rest of the ship or plane, the trim tab can easily go unnoticed even though it is integral to the overall solution. If we look at the trim tab from a perspective of project design and problem solving, we see how easy it can be to miss the most important aspect of a design solution if we are not looking in the right places. As a result, siloed teams that turn hard problems into quick, low cost solutions while excluding UX can never truly design the best solutions because the best solutions are often the most non-obvious. To find them requires observation, collaboration, creativity and a creative, open mindset that allows good design solutions to happen.

> *"[Get] rid of a little nonsense, [get] rid of things that don't work and aren't true until you start to get that trim tab motion. It works every time. That's the grand strategy you're going for."*

> *– R. Buckminster Fuller*

It is not much of a leap to suggest that the UX mindset is our trim tab, an approach that significantly reduces workload, improves efficiency and increases effectiveness. The trim tab may also be the mechanism for turning large, siloed teams into collaborative partners helping to turn large problems into viable solutions that are more efficient, effective and satisfying. This, Fuller said, is the grand strategy we are going for.

In closing, a cautionary tale

> *"Socrates said, "Know thyself." I say, "Know thy users." and guess what? They don't think like you do."*

> *– Josh Brewer, Principal Designer at Twitter*

In this final section, I want to share a cautionary tale, a case study of sorts, about what happens when the UX mindset is ignored and "faster horses" wins out. Unfortunately, this is an all too common scenario that can have serious repercussions.

The story: A pilot purchased an experimental, homemade aircraft and decided to take her up for a short flight. The plane was small, with very little space for the pilot to move around. Here is a photo of a similar plane:

Source: https://upload.wikimedia.org/wikipedia/commons/e/e3/Rutan.variEze.g-veze.arp.jpg

The plane had one previous owner, another pilot who built the plane himself. It was a sparse design that included two gas tanks, one in each wing and a fuel selector valve behind the pilots head to switch between them when one tank was low on fuel.

The cockpit provided very little legroom and no room at all to move around during flight. Because of such tight quarters and to avoid the possibility of a rupturing a fuel line in the event of a belly landing, the plane's builder chose to put the fuel lines behind the pilots head, a change from the original design that called for them to be placed along the cockpit floor. Another change in design was the location of the fuel selector valve. Rather than in front of the pilot, it was placed behind the head and over the left shoulder.

Prior to this particular flight, the pilot and his technician *talked about the inaccessibility of the fuel selector valve and its resistance to being turned*, at one point using a pair of vice grips and a small mirror as a workaround to avoid having to turn and look at it during flight. In retrospect, the plane's original builder was thinking about safety by changing the location of the fuel lines, but in doing so he created a number of critical design flaws. First was the location of the fuel selector and another was not considering an inexperienced in this type of aircraft. The the third was having to interact with a custom-placed fuel selector valve that, by all accounts, was hard to use. Unfortunately, it wasn't long before these flaws made themselves apparent.

As the investigators attempted to recreate the conditions leading up to the crash that took the pilot's life, it didn't take long to figure out what went wrong. The fuel selector valve, a non-obvious problem that the plane's builder never noticed, caused the pilot to extend right foot against the right rudder pedal in order to support body as turned the valve. This put the plane in an unrecoverable spin straight into the Pacific. It was over before the pilot knew what happened.

The aftermath: To call this a mishap a "PICNIC", problem in chair, not in computer, would be incorrect. Those not using a UX mindset might fail to understand that the user will work with what they are given, regardless of the challenges. They may try to compensate with a workaround, but it is the designer who is ultimately responsible for the outcome. Failure to design deliverables with a UX mindset—one's that have been thoroughly tested—can lead to disastrous effects. Now, I am not suggesting that the work of a UX practitioner is life and death, but without a UX mindset it certainly can be when we consider the range of industries in which we can work, such as aviation, hospital emergency room equipment and military technology. In those industries, good design is crucial and can literally be a matter of life and death if we get it wrong.

The user should never notice an interaction or have to think much about it at all. To put it in the simplest of terms, stuff should just work! It should do what the user expects it to do without distraction. Anything less risks failure. Unlike the pilot in this story, we have the opportunity to learn from failure and try again to make it better. Our customers/users rely on that. To ignore them and miss the non-obvious as a result will not be their fault. It is entirely ours. The UX mindset is a muscle that requires attention and usage to get the most out of it and to dispel the myths of "faster horse" thinking for good.

Summary

This chapter introduced the UX mindset, one of the most important concepts you will learn as a UX designer and practitioner and one we will refer back to again and again. We also talked about the myth that listening to our customers/users derails good design and dispelled it using many examples. UX is more than a set of tools, skills, tips and tricks. If we want to be better UX designers and more practical in our approach we first have to acquire the mindset to make it so. UX is a way of viewing the world around you and using it to solve even the most complex and challenging problems, something we will see in later chapters.

Now, let's move on to *Chapter 2, Creative UX*, where we will explore how the UX mindset goes about creating good design.

2
Creative UX

Let's go a little deeper now and talk about another important area of focus for the practical UX practitioner: creativity. Developing a UX mindset is essential to better design work because it allows you to see things differently, which in turn will allow you to design differently, leading to more creative solutions on a consistent basis. Of course, we all want to be our most creative selves most of the time, but in the working world we also have to deal with deadlines, meetings, office politics, and other distractions that can make creativity a major challenge and negatively affect your solutions and subsequent designs. The key, therefore, is to find a balance between creativity and decisiveness, two mindsets or modes that can often be at odds. By following some steps, inspired by someone who knows, you will be able to switch between these two modes more easily and more effectively.

In this chapter, we will look at:

- The essential mindset for creativity
- The six conditions needed for creativity
- Applying creativity to UX design

Essential mindset for Creativity

"Telling people how to be creative is easy; it's only being it that's difficult."

– *John Cleese*

In 1991, comedian and actor John Cleese presented a talk on creativity, providing insight into the creative process along with a recipe for achieving it. Citing research and his own experience as an entertainer, Cleese humorously presented creativity in a very compelling and entertaining way, interspersing his talk with numerous jokes and anecdotes that kept the audience both engaged and thoroughly amused.

During his talk, Cleese emphasized that creativity is not a skill, but rather a "way of operating", and a way of allowing ourselves to be aware and awake to opportunities in any setting and at any moment. Like the UX mindset, creativity is also a way of operating, allowing ideas and solutions to come forth that we might have otherwise missed or misunderstood. This can easily happen in a work setting where we are more often focused on messing up than being messy, which creativity often requires. To better explain this way of thinking/operating, Cleese described creativity, or lack thereof, as a pull between two modes of thought: open and closed. Each absolutely necessary, as long as we use them appropriately and at the right time.

Closed mode

You are probably already familiar with closed mode. It is the mode we often find ourselves in at work when we're thinking about the tasks at hand, the work still to be done, looming deadlines, and the need to get our work completed as quickly and as mistake-free as possible. Closed mode does not allow for creativity, because in the closed mode we have specific goals to accomplish. We have objectives and decisions to make, and we are very focused on the end result. That's not to say creativity isn't happening at some level in closed mode. It is in terms of the work we are doing and what we want the end result to look like, but we often spend far less time being creative and far more time getting to done.

As Cleese described it in his talk:

> "[In closed mode] we have inside us a feeling that there's lots to be done and we have to get on with it if we're going to get through it all. It's an active (probably slightly anxious) mode, although the anxiety can be exiting and pleasurable. It's a mode, which we're probably a little impatient, if only with ourselves. It has a little tension in it, not much humor. It's a mode in which we're very purposeful, and it's a mode in which we can get very stressed and even a bit manic, but not creative."

Open mode

Open mode, by contrast, is much more relaxed, expansive, and less purposeful. In open mode, we are free of deadlines and the stress that comes with finishing and deciding. In open mode, we are in a state of play and have a greater ability to see things from more angles and multiple perspectives. We are also open to anything new that comes our way. In open mode, ideas have less form and more abstract shapes. We are thinking more than doing, and we are more capable of imagining solutions more so than committing them to paper. In open mode ideas and solutions can appear out of nowhere and when we least expect them. In open mode, we are not looking for answers.

We are simply available to receive whatever comes and to decipher that in a more relaxed way. You could say that the UX mindset is very much in the open mode because this is where we need to be for the best solutions to emanate.

> "*[In open mode] we're probably more contemplative, more inclined to humor (which always accompanies a wider perspective) and, consequently, more playful. It's a mood in which curiosity for its own sake can operate because we're not under pressure to get a specific thing done quickly. We can play, and that is what allows our natural creativity to surface.*"
>
> *– John Cleese*

Open and closed modes in action

To give you an example of open and closed modes in action, here is a short story that explains it quite nicely. The year was 1943, and a naval mechanical engineer named Richard James was developing a tension spring that would be used to keep sensitive and delicate shipboard equipment steady, upright, and balanced during rough seas. One day, James accidentally knocked one of the tension springs to the floor. Upon falling, a curious thing happened, as the naval mechanical engineer later recollected.

The falling spring, he explained, "stepped in a series of arcs to a stack of books, to a tabletop, and to the floor, where it re-coiled itself and stood upright." James' discovery would become the Slinky and would go on to become one of the most successful toys in history — *Slinky. From Wikipedia, the free encyclopedia.*

It could have also gone a very different way. Dropping a spring meant for shipboard equipment and seeing what would become a Slinky is a remarkable example of someone most definitely in the open mode, at the precise moment, when it mattered most. However, what would have happened if James had been in closed mode instead? Remember that Richard James was not a toy designer. He was an engineer focused on ship instruments and how to improve their stability in rough seas — not exactly something toy designers spend much time thinking about, at least to the best of my knowledge. Perhaps, rather than seeing an idea for a toy, James had been under pressure to get his work completed. Perhaps, a deadline was looming, and the project was behind or over budget, or a competitor was hard at work, racing to get their version to market first. In that case, dropping a tension spring could have been nothing more than an annoyance. Perhaps, James was feeling impatient and frustrated about a design that just wasn't working as expected. Maybe he was feeling a bit distracted and thinking about other more pressing things that had to get done. Does this sound familiar? It is a state of mind many of us are in while we are attempting to solve hard problems.

It is also an example of the closed mode where we spend much of our brain time at work. In closed mode, James could have simply picked up the spring and continued working, never once stopping to think about what just occurred. How many times have you stopped to contemplate your choices or alternatives to the task at hand? How many opportunities have you missed as a result?

Now, let's contrast this with open mode. In open mode, James is thinking very differently. In open mode, he is feeling open to anything, not encumbered by deadlines and feeling very present. Perhaps, he was so familiar with the work he was doing that he was able to let his mind wander. Perhaps, when the spring dropped, James was in a frame of mind to notice something different, something other than the goal of his work. In closed mode, a tension spring is a tool. In open mode, it's a toy!

Cleese used another story to describe closed and open modes with similar results:

> *"When Alexander Fleming had the thought that led to the discovery of penicillin, he must have been in the open mode. The previous day, he'd arranged a number of dishes so that culture would grow upon them. On the day in question, he glanced at the dishes, and he discovered that on one of them no culture had appeared. Now, if he'd been in the closed mode he would have been so focused upon his need for "dishes with cultures grown upon them" that when he saw that one dish was of no use to him for that purpose he would quite simply have thrown it away. Thank goodness, he was in the open mode so he became curious about why the culture had not grown on this particular dish. And that curiosity, as the world knows, led him to…penicillin."*

To paraphrase Cleese, in the closed mode, an idea or an opportunity can be easily missed because it is irrelevant to what we expected to see. In the open mode, it's a clue! The open mode is where we, as UX practitioners, want to spend most of our time. Open mode is where ideas are formed. It allows us to see the world in a different way. It is arguably where people like Henry Ford, Steve Jobs, Paul MaCready, and Bucky Fuller lived a lot of their time in order to see solutions that nobody else could see. To put it another way, closed mode gave us "faster horses," thinking while open mode gave us the assembly line, affordable automobiles, the iPhone, and the Slinky. Say what you will about these inventions and innovations, but it is hard to make a compelling argument that creativity comes from any other place except our willingness to be open to all ideas and solutions without fear and judgment. In open mode, nothing is out of bounds, and anything is possible, until closed mode brings us back down to earth.

Using open and closed modes together

If open mode is the creative mode, then what good is closed mode and how can we use both to deliver our best work? Cleese explained this very well:

"We need to be in the open mode when we're pondering a problem, but once we come up with a solution, we must then switch to the closed mode to implement it. Because once we've made a decision, we are efficient only if we go through with it decisively, undistracted by doubts about its correctness…Once we've taken a decision we should narrow our focus while we're implementing it, and then after it's been carried out we should once again switch back to the open mode to review the feedback rising from our action, in order to decide whether the course that we have taken is successful, or whether we should continue with the next stage of our plan. Whether we should create an alternative plan to correct any error we perceive. And then back into the closed mode to implement that next stage, and so on."

Switching between the two modes is something we already do naturally. However, it is not something we are often aware of. If we were, we would be able to switch between open and closed modes more easily. To be in such control would allow us tremendous freedom to engage our creative selves more readily. It would also allow us to carve out more time in the day specifically for it. The problem is that we need to remind ourselves to switch modes and sometimes force ourselves to; otherwise, we can become stuck in one for too long. The trick is to know when and how to switch and why to do so.

Stuck in a mode

In a fast-paced work environment where many UX practitioners design, teams can easily find themselves challenged with problems, but where speed to market, siloed team priorities, looming deadlines and tight budgets is the highest priority. This can bring about some significant challenges and problems that leave us stuck in one mode for too long. For example, consider this project scenario:

*   **Setup**: A development team is overseeing a suite of applications and is asked to include a member of the UX team in their next design meeting. This particular project requires an improved interface for an application that helps various clients analyze data related to customer usage and their online business health. The team informs UX that users have been complaining about the readability of the information presented on screen and also have been asking that content be better organized and more easily located. Another feature of the interface is a dashboard where users can see data in an aggregated format more quickly. The problem is that the dashboard graphics are not immediately understandable, and users are not sure what they are looking at or how to decipher the information presented. As a result, customers/users are spending a lot of time on the phone with customer support. The problem has gotten so bad that the development team and the product sponsor are considering removing the dashboard functionality altogether.

○ **Next step**: The UX designer listens carefully to the problems presented and schedules a follow-up meeting pending their review of the current application and requesting interviews with a variety of end users to uncover any non-obvious issues or unforeseen opportunities. Additional meetings are also scheduled with stakeholders to understand business goals, and to ask the hard questions as seen in *Chapter 1, The User Experience Mindset* to identify how to measure and prove our success. Meetings are also scheduled with the development team to understand some of the back end challenges and possible limitations to our potential design solution. The developers decline the meeting citing more pressing deadlines. The stakeholder requests a half-hour meeting instead of an hour. Frustrated and somewhat dispirited, the UX designer agrees in order to keep the project moving forward.

- **The Meeting**: With only a half hour to discuss the issues, metrics and potential obstacles, there is little hope that all of that will get accomplished. The UX designer begins asking questions around **key performance indicators (KPIs)** and business goals, but nobody has the necessary data to provide answers. The meeting ends with little being accomplished. The UX designer is asked to just look at the requirements and design something that the development team can review and begin coding because, of course, this has to be rolled out in the very near future.

○ **Next steps**: With little time to think about the problems and their root causes and even less time to fully understand the business goals of the project, the UX designer retreats to their desk and spends the next two days sketching possible solutions as options for the team to consider. With deadlines looming, the UX designer wants to be as creative as possible. They schedule a meeting room to work in, away from distractions such as ringing phones, e-mails, and work requests from other colleagues. With time running out and worry setting in, the UX designer delivers what they feel is their best work given the time, but they really know it is average at best. They hope that the project team doesn't notice.

Have you ever been in a situation like this? In reality, this is a very common scenario where UX is provided very little information, less data, and if we are lucky, minimal cooperation or time from the people we need to be most involved and engaged. In situations like this, it is easy to get stuck in closed mode rather than trying to be truly creative. There simply isn't enough information or time to do anything else. You may think you are being creative with what you have and you may be.

However, in reality, our truly best work can only come when we are not in delivery mode. Open mode requires a relaxed environment where stress and the need to make quick decisions are avoided.

In closed mode, Cleese noted that we have no other choice but to " narrow our focus while we're implementing it." Only after the crisis has been averted can we even begin to be in open mode where we can

"review the feedback rising from our action, in order to decide whether the course that we have taken is successful or whether we should continue with the next stage of our plan...or create an alternative plan to correct any error we perceive."

Closed mode allows us to think on our feet in a very practical way in order to avoid any danger. When we are under pressure, we tend to narrow our options and maintain tunnel vision at the time when we should be taking a step back to contemplate the problem from a much wider view.

Consider those with whom you work. Does your manager seem to be in a constant state of panic, always reacting and putting out fires? Not only are they stuck in closed mode, but they expect everyone around them to be too. Being stuck in open mode can be a problem too. Too much thinking and not enough doing, when everyone around you is in closed mode, risks the appearance of being disengaged and not displaying a sense of urgency needed to get things done. As much as you want to be highly creative, at some point, decisions have to be made.

Becoming unstuck in either mode requires certain conditions to be met, conditions that are necessary for closed and open modes to work together. It is important to note too that being in open mode does not guarantee creativity. It simply guarantees that if you create the proper conditions you would, at the very least, have created the best opportunity for your most creative self to flourish.

The six conditions for creativity

What follows are six conditions necessary to obtain optimal creativity and getting to the open mode when you need it the most. As you will see, although they were not intended for a UX designer, they transfer nicely. Also note that while Cleese introduced five conditions during his talk, a sixth one has been added (agreement), because in a work oriented project setting, if you do not have an agreement about what the business and customer/user goals and objectives are then the other conditions are irrelevant. I will explain more about this in a moment.

The six conditions for optimal creativity and getting to open mode are as follows:

- **Space**: Finding the physical space to be creative
- **Time**: Putting aside time for creativity to occur
- **Time**: Allowing yourself enough time to be creative
- **Confidence**: Knowing when to switch between open and closed modes
- **Humor**: Allowing for and embracing failure
- **Agreement**: Gaining an agreement that your approach is sound

Space

If we search Google to look for images using the keyword "creativity," it returns images of the brain, denoting internal and cerebral thoughts, deep contemplation, and concentration. There are also images of a single light bulb, depicting the moment when a brilliant idea occurs. Other images depict people with their eyes closed or just a multitude of brilliant colors. Replicating this experience in real life can mean finding a quiet place to reflect in order for deep thoughts to occur. It is also a place where we are most free to let out imaginations run wild. We even call them "spaces".

Musicians have rehearsal space, painters have an art studio space, chefs have spacious kitchens, and so on. What does a UX designer have? Where is our physical space where distractions are at a minimum and where we can be at our most creative? In a work environment we often have to make our own. No matter, the requirements are the same:

- No phones.
- No e-mail.
- No computers, unless for presenting and taking notes.
- No clock watching.
- No judgment! We are not our ideas. We are simply allowing ideas to come to us and through us. Failure is encouraged, so long as we are trying!

These rules are very simple and you might be thinking this is obvious, but how often are you really allowing for creativity?

> *"It's easier to do trivial things that are urgent than it is to do important things that are not urgent, like thinking…it's also easier to do little things we know we can do, than to start on big things that we're not so sure about."*
>
> *– John Cleese*

One other thing to ask yourself, how open are you and your team to working on a problem until it is truly solved, rather than feeling the urge to just get it done and move on? As we will see next, time is key. Now only making time to be creative, but also allowing for the time to do it. You may never have noticed, but the next time you are being creative and feeling like you are in open mode, think about how you feel when good ideas are not coming fast enough. Being in open mode can actually make you feel physically ill, forcing you to want to finish in order to feel better. Don't be tricked. Time is a requirement.

Time

Think about the last time you were in a creative open mindset. Did time seem to fly by? Did hours seem like minutes? Juxtapose this with how it feels when you are rushing through a project with deadlines looming. Time goes by too, but much more slowly. In closed mode you are thinking about a lot about time and perhaps even looking at the clock as you sweat it out to get finished. The result of this experience is often substandard work that can leave you feeling mildly depressed and thinking if you only you had a little more time, how much better your work could have been. Of course, oftentimes making time at work is a luxury.

As Cleese pointed out:

> *"It's not enough to create space; you have to create your space for a specific period of time. You have to know that your space will last until exactly (say) 3:30, and that at that moment your normal life will start again."*

Just be sure to book time when deadlines aren't looming. An hour in open mode is far better than none at all. Of course, booking time for creativity can be a challenge too. However, it is amazing how you can magically find time when doing something very enjoyable, like creating, designing and solving problems.

Time – again

The next condition is also time, but rather than finding time to be creative, this "time" means taking your time to be creative. You may be wondering, how to do this? We're all busy during the day! How long is this going to take? It's a great question and the answer depends on you and the problem(s) at hand. Some people need an hour, while others need a whole day or more. Sometimes, you can spend a week and nothing will come, while some days, you accidentally drop a tension spring and a Slinky appears. How long creativity takes is different for everyone. However, without making time on a regular basis and exercising your open mode muscle, you can be sure that it will never come. To put it in the simplest terms, make enough time for "your mind to quiet down," without distractions and without the need to suddenly switch back to closed mode.

If in that time nothing comes, don't worry. There's always next time, as long as you continue to make time for a next time. Also, if you are working with a team, it could be far more productive to break up creative sessions into multiple ones over multiple days rather than trying to cram creativity into a single marathon session. You may also find that leaving your ideas in the room and returning to them later—be it hours, days, or even weeks—can provide fresh insight and greater opportunity to move forward more productively when you return. The worst thing to do in these situations is to rush to conclusions just to get it over with. Don't ruin the opportunity for great ideas to come simply because you want to move on.

> *"The people I find it hardest to be creative with are people who need all the time to project an image of themselves as decisive and who feel that to create this image they need to decide everything very quickly and with a great show of confidence. Well, this behavior I suggest sincerely, is the most effective way of strangling creativity at birth."*
>
> *– John Cleese*

Another tendency people have is to become impatient with others who are taking longer to get to a solution, creating a feeling of "internal agitation, tension, or an uncertainty that makes us just plain uncomfortable." When this happens and to avoid this feeling, we quickly jump to conclusions and make decisions. If you see this happening to you or someone around you, stop! Don't be a decider in the open mode. Instead, trust that a solution will come so long as you allow it to.

The 10,000 hour rule

To give you a better grasp of time and what could be needed for creativity, I will share a personal story of life in the open mode. I am a drummer and have been for most of my life. This is me, in a moment of creativity and pure joy:

Playing an instrument at a level where it can be done in the company of others and sound good is not only thoroughly satisfying and highly recommended, but it is also a major accomplishment that began years earlier. Going back to my earliest days as a drummer, I can remember blisters and callousness on my hands and fingers, hearing complaints by my parents about how loud the noise was, and being rejected many times at auditions, for one reason or another. Was it hurtful? Yes. Did it discourage me? Sometimes. Did I quit? Never! Why? Because the act of learning, practicing, playing and working through problems were small, compared to performing and seeing myself become a better musician as a result.

Playing an instrument may look easy, but it actually requires years of dedicated practice. A famous quote by Pablo Casals, one of the world's greatest cellists, continued to practice his instrument into his 90's. When asked why he said: "Because I think I am making some progress." Of course, getting to a mastery level can take a lifetime, and even then, there is no guarantee. Malcolm Gladwell, in his book *Outliers*, wrote that "the magic number" to acquire greatness in anything is 10,000 hours. Now, to be clear, Gladwell was not suggesting that this number makes someone a champion or famous or even the best, for that matter.

The point Gladwell was making, as he stated in an interview, was that "natural ability requires a huge investment of time in order to be made manifest." — *Malcolm Gladwell Explains What Everyone Gets Wrong About His Famous '10,000 Hour Rule'*, businessinsider.com, *June, 2014*. For musicians and athletes and UX designers, becoming highly proficient and highly creative takes time and often a good deal of discomfort. You will find, however, that the most creative people would not trade it for anything in the world, because once they arrive, any discomfort they may have experienced pales in comparison to the payoff.

> *"I fear not the man who has practiced 10,000 kicks once, but I fear the man who has practiced one kick 10,000 times."*

> *– Bruce Lee*

By jumping to conclusions and making quick decisions, we are essentially trying to get around the "ten thousand hour rule" and trying to get lucky, much the same way lottery players spend time scratching a card instead of focusing on a tangible goal that can have a much more rewarding payoff—perhaps not monetarily speaking, but in a more substantial and longer lasting way. This is precisely what we could accomplish for our customers/users if we truly take the time to design and deliver highly creative solutions that solve the right problems. Now, this is not to suggest that we need 10,000 hours to do it, but unless we are willing to put in at least enough time to experience some discomfort and then move beyond it, we will never truly know what possibilities exist on the other side.

Confidence

> *"When you are in your space/time oasis, getting into the open mode, nothing will stop you being creative so effectively as the fear of making a mistake."*

> *– John Cleese*

This next condition is an interesting one because with discomfort often comes the fear that no matter how hard we try, we still feel like we are failing. For example, many of us know that public speaking can be one of the scariest experiences. In fact, it usually rates higher than our fear of dying in terms of things we are most afraid of. In other words, we would rather die than get up in front of a room full of people and say something stupid, look silly, freeze or perhaps not even be able to utter a word. How horrifying! We also fear being judged. It is as if everyone is watching us from a safe distance and as a result they seem superior or smarter because they are not currently risking it all by getting up on stage. In these situations, we even feel that those watching actually want us to fail!

Interestingly though, the exact opposite is true. Think about this the next time someone gets up to speak in front of you. Do you want them to fail? Chances are you want them to succeed because you want to be informed and not bored to tears with another PowerPoint presentation and told things you already know or don't really care about. You want the person speaking to be knowledgeable, interesting, engaging and creative, because this is far more entertaining. If only the audience would convey this, perhaps public speaking would be something more people wanted to do.

Fear can stop creativity in its tracks. On the other hand, fear is also a great motivator that builds confidence when we realize there was nothing to be afraid of. Trying to be creative in a team setting can be fear inducing as well. Is your idea dumb? Will people ignore it or counter with something they feel is better? No matter. To be in the open mode requires fearlessness. Anyone who is judging or seeming impatient is a "decider" who should not be in the room at all or told to get out of the closed mode so we can actually find the right solution. Confidence is not being afraid of failing and then getting back up when you do. This is also the best time to fail because once you are out on that stage, it is too late.

In a study performed by a team of scientists at Johns Hopkins University, six Jazz piano players were asked to improvise some music while hooked up to an MRI. The aim of the study was to understand how the brain works as we create. The study found that:

> *"The parts of the frontal lobe associated with judgment went quiet. This shows that while self-monitoring is often useful — you don't want to say everything that passes through your mind — it can get in the way of new ideas."*
>
> *– Drake Baer, Why Humor Makes You More Creative,* fastcompany.com

Play

Not surprisingly, creative people can turn off the part of the brain that passes judgment in order to allow more ideas to pass through. There is also a correlation between play — be it on an instrument, in a schoolyard, or on a project team — and creativity. In another study, participants, ranging from students to professional designers to improvisational comedians, were given a "cartoon caption humor test." The study found that the comedians "generated 20 percent more ideas than professional product designers…and the comedians generated ideas that were also rated 25 percent more creative." — *The Power of Humor in Ideation and Creativity,* psychologytoday.com, *June, 2014.*

Consider the products, websites and mobile apps you have designed. Were they successful? How do you know? What criteria did you use to find out? More importantly, based on the level of success, how much fun did you have creating them? Once again, science shows a direct correlation:

> *"Research by Mark Beeman and John Kounios...found that participants who watched clips of Robin Williams doing stand-up experienced more epiphanies than participants who watched scary movies or boring videos. Moreover, a study published in 2010 by researchers at the University of Western Ontario found that participants who watched a video of a laughing baby and listened to Mozart were better at recognizing a pattern."*

> *– How Your Mood Affects Your Creativity,* `bigthink.com.`

Remember that creativity is serious business. The least you can do is enjoy it!

Agreement

Now that you have met all the conditions for creativity to occur in the open mode, the final step is agreement:

- Agreement from the entire project team to work together for as long as it takes to find the right solution

- Agreement on a solution

- Agreement from our stakeholders that we are focusing on the right metrics and measurements and agreement on how we will track our success

- Agreement from our customers/users that we are focusing on the right problems and that our solution is to their satisfaction

If we do not have agreement in these areas, then anything we create or try to create will be insufficient at best. Creativity only works when we remove the silos and come together with a singular purpose to design solutions that are best for everyone involved.

Applying creativity to UX design

Now that we've looked at creativity and the conditions necessary to manifest it, let's see how they hold up in real-world work environments where speed, efficiency, and decision making are the highest priority, sometimes higher than the concern for customer/user satisfaction. In other words, how do we create the open mode in an environment designed for closed mode thinking most of the time?

To visualize this, here are two images that come to mind with regards to closed and open modes. Can you guess which is which?

In the preceding image, development teams are focused on efficiency, production, and deadlines more so than on customer/user needs.

Here is another image:

Here we see creativity personified, where the conditions for being in the open mode seem to come to life all at once. In this image there appears to be a playful, cohesive team in a dedicated space where play and improvisation abounds. There also appears to be total freedom to try, test, imagine, and innovate with, one would assume, plenty of confidence and little judgment.

Nevertheless, the reality is that despite the two extremes depicted in these images, both require the open and closed modes to co-exist, otherwise in the fist image innovation cannot take place and in the bottom image, nothing concrete and decisive will ever get done. It is a delicate balance between them and one that requires constant awareness and attention to make sure both can co-exist in order for the most mature teams to produce and deliver the highest quality products.

The space between

If you find yourself in an environment where open and closed mode thinking are at odds to the detriment of your deliverables, here are some important points to remember:

- Share your approach to problem solving with your team and walk them through the conditions, presented here, that are necessary for creativity to take place. Try this approach on a small scale at first then learn and build from there.

- Learn as much as you can about what your team is working on and the problems they face before you get together to work through it. Do your homework and come prepared. Meet with stakeholders to understand their business goals and vision. Help them determine the best metrics for success. Being knowledgeable in their space will go a long way to building the trust necessary to allow the freedom for the open mode to exist.

- Create a space for creativity, even if it is not a dedicated one. Book a room for 90 minutes and invite members of your project team to talk about the problems at hand. Be a facilitator and a leader in the space. Challenge your team to think outside of their comfort zone. When the pain and discomfort comes, help them through it and remind them that the feeling will pass. Don't give in to it. Push on ahead!

- Provide an agenda for the creative sessions prior to the meeting, if need be, and time box it. Then, follow up afterwards with the notes captured, recapping what was discussed, what was learned, progress made, and the next steps.

- Create teams of like-minded people who understand what you are all trying to accomplish. Avoid "deciders" at all costs!

- Replace negativity with positivity when interacting in the open mode space. Use phrases such as "Yes!", "I like that, but…", "Let's imagine…", "It might be fun to try…", and so on.

- Most importantly, have fun!

Summary

"Anything looked at closely becomes wonderful."

– A. R. Ammons

In this chapter, we looked at the essential mindset for creativity, the six conditions needed for creativity and applying creativity to UX design. Facilitating creativity in a work-/team-oriented environment more often steeped in efficiency, production, and deadlines than on customer/user needs can be a real problem. Inspired by a talk on creativity by actor/comedian John Cleese, we looked at two modes of thinking, open and closed and how to switch between them in order to be both creative and productive. We looked to at how getting stuck in either of these modes risks missed opportunities and less than superior results. Creativity and decision making is a balancing act that is important to understand and be aware of in our professional lives. Making time and space for creativity is key and can be easily accomplished by following the conditions introduced by Mr. Cleese, which transfer nicely to UX design. Finally, we looked at how to incorporate open and closed mode thinking into our every day work experience and company culture and how to make space for serious decision making in a space conducive for UX to play within.

Creativity is a process through which our imagination can travel. It is where experimentation and ideas either succeed or fail, safely and without judgment. It is also a place where teams unfamiliar with the open mode can be drawn in and where they too can stretch, think, and play, and ultimately agree on the best path forward. Make space, make time, be confident, gain agreement, but above all, enjoy the journey!

3
Good UX Design

"With the passage of time, the psychology of people stays the same, but the tools and objects in the world change."

– Donald A. Norman, The Design of Everyday Things.

Design is what we deliver at the end of the day after all of the research, brainstorming, team meetings, requirements, solutions, wireframing, prototyping, usability testing, and iterating has been done. However, how do we know whether what we've delivered is good? From an aesthetic perspective, it's difficult to say what good design is, because good design is not easily identifiable. In fact, it is quite hard to identify because it is often very subjective. For example, one person may love an iPhone while another swears that an Android phone is better. This used to happen with Macs and PCs too, but Apple makes a better machine and the competition simply can't compete. Then again, you might disagree.

In this chapter we will:

- Explore the concept of "good" design
- Present and explore ten principles of good design
- Learn by examples to help you identify and create good design

Becoming a UX leader means knowing the principles of good design and how to identify and create good design in your own work. As you will see, learning from great designers and designs will sharpen your understanding of design, enabling greater focus on what matters most.

What is good design?

For a designer of any kind, subjectivity is one of the hardest things to overcome when designing for other people. It is much easier to design what *we* want than to ask our customers/users what *they* want. When a design is subjective, it is often based on nothing more than our opinion, and we can easily mistake our opinion for that of our customers/users. When this happens, problems can occur.

Consider, for example, the mindset of a designer who has knowledge and expertise in a specific area. Perhaps, they prefer one type of interaction to another. Perhaps, that same interaction would seem confusing to someone else. What seems easy or second nature to one person can be totally incomprehensible to another. Think of a musician who has been playing the guitar for a number of years compared to someone who is just learning to play. The experienced musician cannot remember what it was like when they first learned to play all those years ago. What seems simple to them now would seem impossible to a beginner. This holds true for designers as well. There is a phrase often used to describe this problem of designing without an outsider's perspective. It's called *being inside the bubble*. It means we have been involved with an idea or concept for so long that we have become insulated from critique. To get around this, we look to outsiders to give us a fresh perspective. This is why usability testing is so valuable. It allows us to see outside, unbiased reactions to our work by those who are seeing it for the first time. It is from this perspective that we are able to see where improvements are needed. It is also the moment when the customer/user essentially *pops our bubble* and brings us back to reality, where we can improve our design before we deliver it.

Good design is non-obvious

To understand how to identify good design, let's begin with a simple example. Amazon is often used as the go-to for good design for many reasons. For one, when you go to their website, it is immediately obvious what they are. Early on, Amazon sold books exclusively, and they were quite well-known for this. Today, Amazon has an expansive business model that incorporates much more than just books. Need a goat for grazing? Amazon has you covered.

Source: Amazon.com, Home Services

However, knowing this, does it change your understanding of Amazon? If you look back to how Amazon looked in 2001, do you really notice a difference from today?

This was Amazon in 2001:

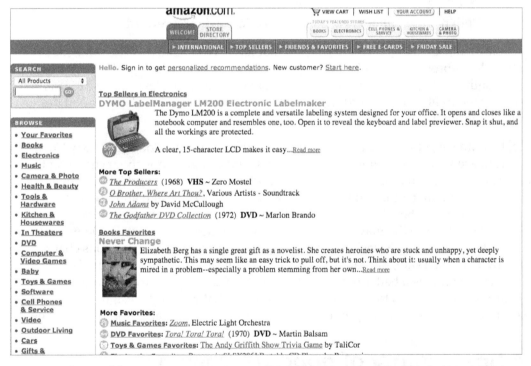

Source: http://www.exacttarget.com/blog/wp-content/uploads/2014/08/
screen_shot_2014-08-05_at_1.18.31_pm2.png

They had fewer items in 2001, and the design looks dated, but if Amazon suddenly returned to this earlier design, would you be confused by it? Would you suddenly be unsure what to do or how to make a purchase? Has Amazon really changed that much since 2001? Sure, they have improved their appearance, made purchasing easier and faster, and sell just about anything you can think of, but have they really changed? The more important question is did they really need to?

In terms of essential design elements, let's compare 2001 Amazon to today:

- They are both well organized
- They both lead our eye to the correct places
- They both use natural language that is immediately understandable
- They both deliver on our expectations
- Neither requires a lot of thinking
- Both require minimal effort and provide maximum reward

In a nutshell, Amazon represents design that has stayed relatively the same for over a decade, improved simply by adding more features as technology allowed. It has also continued to provide its customers/users with the same level of ease of use, understandability, and rewarding experience since its inception. This is good design, and this is what UX designers need to achieve in their design work as well.

So, how do we get there? Can we all be as good as Amazon, Google, or eBay? Yes, we can, even if it is on a much smaller scale. Good design is not about changing the world. Good design is about providing a solid foundation from which to grow. It is ironic, though, that although we are exposed to good UX design and use it everyday, we still manage to fall short more often than not in terms of our own work or the work of our teams who may be trying but failing to design effectively. Do we lack the skills to be good UX designers? If you recall a quote from the previous chapter, creativity is not a skill, but rather *"a way of operating."* This holds true for UX design too. Anyone can be a better designer, but good UX design requires the right mindset in addition to allow us to become more aware of what good UX design is when we see it, not from a subjective point of view, but from a view that is not up for debate.

A brief history of good UX design

When the Internet and the World Wide Web first appeared and before UX became a recognized, professional skill, design was often the job of visual designers and/or developers. The goal early on was to present something that looked nice and that got the attention of the viewer. In those days, it was all very experimental. Nobody was really sure what a good user experience was or what it was supposed to look like. Those that did understand evolved and grew quickly.

For example, here's eBay in 1996:

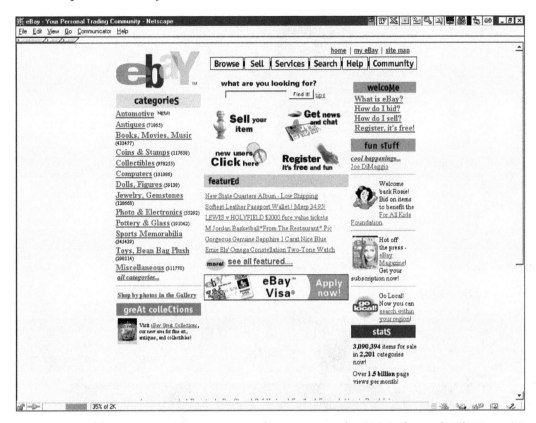

Source: http://www.jamesaltucher.com/wp-content/uploads/2012/06/ebay.gif

It may look retro now, but back then, most people had no trouble turning this site into a major player in online sales.

Here's Google in 1998:

Source: https://annietv600.files.wordpress.com/2008/02/googledec98.png

This is CNN in 2010:

Source: http://www.thejavajive.com/images/blog/CNN.png

Have they all changed a lot? Perhaps, aesthetically they have, but not dramatically. They actually look relatively similar and are easily identifiable in any incarnation. They are also as popular today as they once were, precisely because they got it right the first time by designing an interface that was understandable, enjoyable, and valuable for the customer/user.

With so many examples to show us what makes for good design, why does bad UX design still exist? How is it that designers and developers rely so heavily on good design with their iPhones, Androids, and other technology used everyday, all day, but still deliver solutions that are not easily understood, at least not without a manual, special training or a call to the help desk?

Good design is invisible

"Good design is actually a lot harder to notice than poor design, in part because good designs fit our needs so well that the design is invisible."

– Donald A. Norman, The Design of Everyday Things

As UX designers, we know we have done our job when our customers/users feel empowered, confident, and above all, intelligent. This may sound funny, but it's not a joke. Think about what good design does for you in your life. Do you ponder over the design of your coffee maker in the morning? What about your washing machine? Do you think much about the design of your GPS application as you are driving at night in an unfamiliar city? These are everyday interactions that we take for granted, because when design is good, we simply don't notice.

Think about that the next time you are driving. Whether it's a Porsche or a Prius, aside from the features, both do the exact same thing. Turn it on, and both will take you to your destination with little thought on how to do it. The steering wheel is where you expect it to be, so are the gas and brake pedals. Sure, the Porsche may have additional features and provide a totally different driving experience, but the basic solution to the problem (getting from point A to point B) is the same. Change that in any way, and the design fails. Why? Because when basic expectations are moved, missing, or changed, they suddenly become apparent, and when our customers/users notice it, it means we failed.

Good design creates emotion

"Cognition attempts to make sense of the world: emotion assigns value."

– Donald A. Norman, The Design of Everyday Things.

Think about how you feel when something doesn't work like it should. Do you feel angry? Frustrated? Stupid? What about when it does? You probably feel empowered, smart and tech savvy. How we react to design and how it makes us feel when we interact with it plays a big part in how good the design is, and it doesn't have to be complex design either. If you are old like me, you may remember the movie, *National Lampoon's Vacation*. When I was writing this chapter a scene from that movie popped into my head. It is the scene where Clark, played by Chevy Chase, pulls into a gas station to fill up. He's driving a new car, and apparently up to this point he has not had to put gas into the tank. As Clark proceeds to pump the gas, the car's gas tank is not where he expected it to be.

 Follow this link to view this scene on YouTube:
`https://www.youtube.com/watch?v=MxTQT9LmzTY`
or type into Google: `national lampoon's vacation gas station`.

As Clark continues his search for the gas tank, he spies another customer about to fill up their tank, which is located behind the license plate. Nope, no fuel tank there either. How could something as simple as the fuel tank be so hard to find? When Clark's wife returns to the car she offhandedly discovers the gas tank in an inexplicably odd place – in the hood of the car! It is a place most people, including Clark, would never think to look.

The scene gets a laugh because not only could Clark not find the tank, but when it *was* found, it was in a location so unexpected that it was considered funny by the writers. Do you want your design to make people laugh or cause frustration because of how absurd it is or would you rather make them feel empowered, smart, or better yet, feeling nothing at all? Sometimes, not eliciting an emotion is a sign of success too. Anything less and your customers/users might blame themselves for something that is simply not their fault. As this scene demonstrated, changing the location of something or just making something harder than it needs to be, can be a frustrating and even an embarrassing experience for the user.

Our goal as designers is to elicit positive reaction, which we can see through repeated use, improved business results and positive feedback. Good design creates a feeling of control and empowerment and solves problems. It should never create them. Fail at this and even the most mundane and trivial problems become enough to make us very emotional.

Source: `http://klipd.com/screenshots/48e854abf6fdf64ca6812bf6cc6cd9` `4b-1.jpg`

 What is he about to hit with that bat? Follow this link to find out: `https://www.youtube.com/watch?v=pD2xBXm4y70&nohtml` `5=False`
Or Google: `office space printer`

Good design is familiar

I own a Prius, a car that delivers on its promise of great fuel efficiency. It's also very dependable and offers a comfortable ride. Being a hybrid, the thought of driving this type of car created some questions in my mind. Would it drive like a regular car? Would it be powerful enough on the highway? Is it safe to drive? All these concerns were immediately put to rest the moment I drove it because the Prius, it turns out, is a very well-conceived and well-designed driving experience. There are, nevertheless, a few aspects of the design that could be better. For example, the Prius has a park button:

Source: `http://simplyrides.com/wp-content/uploads/2011/06/toyota-prius-interior-button-control-4dddc96c2cfa2.jpg`

Being an older driver, a park button is a new interaction. Prior to this, putting a car into park was done using the gearshift. There have been multiple occasions where I mindlessly pushed the gearshift forward thinking that I was in park only to have to quickly hit the brake to avoid hitting the car in front of me. Another issue with the Prius is that it has an engine that is totally silent. In fact, engine technology has becomes so sophisticated that engine noise is becoming a thing of the past. Interestingly, customers still expect it, so car manufactures made a compromise; they replaced real engine noise with a digital version:

> *"Enhanced engine songs have become the signature of eerily quiet electrics such as the Toyota Prius. But the fakery is increasingly finding its way into beefy trucks and muscle cars, long revered for their iconic growl."*

> – `https://www.washingtonpost.com/business/economy/americas-best-selling-cars-and-trucks-are-built-on-lies-the-rise-of-fake-engine-noise/`

The Prius engine is so quiet that I once forget to turn it off! The car attempted to warn me of this mistake with a series of quiet beeps that sounded like the car locking. If you are not familiar with these sounds and didn't read the owner's manual, it is easy to ignore. I realized my mistake only after I returned 8 hours later!

The reason for bringing this up is not to sell you a Prius, but to demonstrate how familiarity plays a part in good design and how changing it can affect your user's experience. Consider the repercussions of your solutions and test them with real customers/users to gauge their experience and emotions. Then, decide whether the change was worth it. Remember, just because something appears to be a good design and an improvement to an existing problem, it doesn't mean it is. Put it to the test with real users and find out.

When preference beats performance

In the case of the Prius, changing a few familiar design elements is acceptable because most drivers are more interested in fuel efficiency. Nevertheless, this can also go the other way when changes intended to improve design are not necessarily what users want or prefer, even if they supposedly benefit them. A good example of this can be found with the computer keyboard layout called QWERTY. It gets its name because of the first five letter keys on the computer keyboard. QWERTY was originally designed for typewriters to place "common two-letter combinations on opposite sides of the keyboard" in order to avoid the keys sticking together. If you've never used a typewriter, this might be hard to visualize, but regardless, the QWERTY layout became the standard and has never changed. The problem with QWERTY, however, is that it was believed to decrease typing speed and increase typing errors, due to the unnatural location of the keys.

In the early twentieth century, an educational psychologist and professor named August Dvorak designed an alternate layout to QWERTY that he claimed would decrease typing errors, speed up typing, and lessen typing fatigue. He called his design the Dvorak Simplified Keyboard and had 70 percent *of the most commonly used letters in the home row*, while QWERTY had only 32 percent. Nevertheless, whatever improvements Dvorak promised were not enough to outweigh the negatives, such as the time required to learn a new layout, the fact that typing was already a complicated physical activity, and more importantly that nobody was really complaining about the current layout. This is an important tip to remember. Your research is not complete until you talk to and observe your customers/users, and discover the problems they are having. If you fail to do so or if you do this and find that nobody is complaining, you may also find that your so-called *improved* design solution fails to catch on— https://en.wikipedia.org/wiki/Dvorak_Simplified_Keyboard.

Here are the two keyboard layouts for comparison:

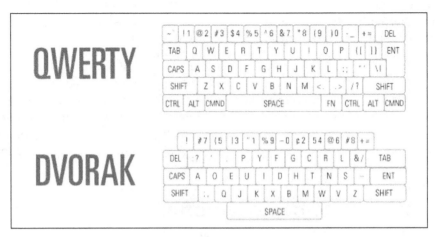

Source: http://www.blogcdn.com/www.switched.com/media/2010/09/keyboard.jpg

The Dvorak keyboard showed improvements in the areas claimed, but while many companies preferred the new layout to improve the typing efficiency of their staff, the actual users weren't willing to change because they were not experiencing any difficulty with the current version. If they were, they really didn't mind. Add to this the time required to retrain staff on the Dvorak layout and nobody was willing to change.

When you are designing solutions, it is important to remember that for people to engage and be willing to learn something new, the reasons must be compelling enough to do so and based on an observed need. Don't waste time solving problems that do not exist or ones you think should be different based on your own personal preference or just because the data says so. Oftentimes, the data can be misleading. Good design requires creative thinking to understand what the data is really telling you. We will look at this more closely when we review the case studies in *Chapter 6, An Essential Strategy for UX Maturity.*

To recap, here are some rules to help guide your design decisions:

- Understand the data, the business goals and your customers/users needs before sketching or drawing solutions
- Design the right solution to solve the right problem
- Ask questions such as who wants our solution and how will they benefit?
- Just because you can design something doesn't mean you should
- Listen to what your customers/users say, verify through observation, test with potential users, and then validate your findings
- Follow proven principles of good design

The principles of good design

A poorly-designed product is not only uglier than a well-designed one but it is of less value and use. Worst of all it might be intrusive.

– Dieter Rams

Remember the time when banner ads were everywhere? Remember how they used to blink and obstruct your view continue opening on screen until you had to literally close your browser to make them stop? These types of ads may no longer exist, but ads are still very much with us, replaced by clever advertising that we are often not even aware exists. Perhaps, you have seen them. Here is an example:

Source: http://www.wordstream.com/blog/ws/2014/07/07/native-advertising-examples

Did you spot the ad in the image above? It is not easy to see, especially if you are not looking for it. That's because this is a form of advertising, called "native advertising," designed to look exactly like the rest of the content on the page. Native advertising has become so prevalent that CNN created its own in-house studio exclusively to produce native advertising campaigns, "a move that reflects marketers' growing desire for articles and videos that feel like editorial work." — `http://blogs.wsj.com/cmo/2015/06/08/cnn-courageous-branded-content-studio/`.

If you are still not sure, the arrow below points to the "native" advertisement:

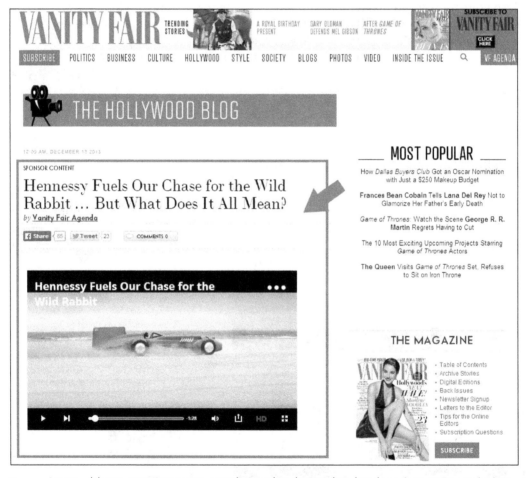

Source: `http://www.wordstream.com/blog/ws/2014/07/07/native-advertising-examples`

Have a look at `http://www.wordstream.com/blog/ws/2014/07/07/native-advertising-examples`. Native advertising is meant to fool the user into clicking in order to increase revenue . It's very clever, seemingly non-intrusive, and almost invisible design, but is it good design? It's a great question and one we'll come back to later in the chapter after we've taken a closer look at some of the principles of good design.

Good design is timeless

In the late 1970s, influential German designer Dieter Rams had become *increasingly concerned by the state of the world around him.* — `https://readymag.com/shuffle/dieter-rams/intro/`.

> *I imagine our current situation will cause future generations to shudder at the thoughtlessness in the way in which we today fill our homes, our cities and our landscape with a chaos of assorted junk. What a fatalistic apathy we have towards the effect of such things. What atrocities we have to tolerate. Yet we are only half aware of them…This complex situation is increasing and possibly irreversible: there are no discrete actions anymore. Everything interacts and is dependent on other things; we must think more thoroughly about what we are doing, how we are doing it and why we are doing it.*

> `-www.vitsoe.com/files/assets/1000/17/VITSOE_`
`Dieter_Rams_speech.pdf`

Out of his concerns for the state of design and its future, Rams introduced the *Ten Principles of a Good Design* that still hold true today and transfer nicely to the realm of UX.

According to Rams, the principles of good design are as follows:

- Innovative
- Useful
- Minimalist
- Understandable
- Valuable*
- Safe
- Long lasting
- Aesthetically pleasing
- Unobtrusive
- Honest
- Thorough

We'll review some of these principles through examples, but first, we need to note a few things:

- The principles are not numbered because the order can change based on your design priorities.

- I will provide examples of the first six principles in the order of how they appear in this list.

- Rams originally titled the principle referred to as "safe" as "environment-friendly." Since these principles were written prior to the Internet, I created Safe as an alternative title more appropriate in our current context.

- If you counted the 10 principles and found 11 of them, this is not a mistake. I added one (valuable). You will understand why in the pages that follow.

Principles of good UX design, by example

> *"Products fulfilling a purpose are like tools. They are neither decorative objects nor works of art."*
>
> *– Dieter Rams*

What follows are examples of good UX design as they align to the principles Rams suggested. They were chosen not for their popularity, but because they most closely adhered to the design principles. Use these examples to compare against your designs. Use them as a checklist too to ensure that you are adhering to these principles and meeting the basic standards of *good* design. Remember that these examples are for demonstration purposes. As you review, think about the designs you like and see whether/how these principles stand up in comparison. Talk about them with your classmates and/or colleagues. Above all, use them!

Innovative

The following image is of a device you may be familiar with. It's a first generation iPod. If you've never owned one, you may be wondering why the screen is so small or how to move things around. Compared to the devices we use today, it looks simply archaic! Then again, this was a long time ago. The first iPod came out in 2001 and was quite simply the most amazing device money could buy. Holding one in your hand was quite literally like holding the future! Here's an image of the first generation iPod:

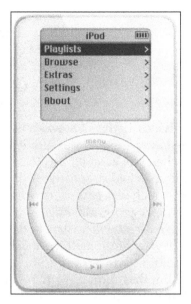

Source: http://www.technobuffalo.com/wp-content/uploads/2010/03/first-gen-ipod.jpg

This tiny device could hold up to 1,000 songs. Nothing like it had ever existed before. Within a month and a half of its release, Apple sold 125,000 iPods. Three years later, this number increased to 2 million. The iPod literally changed the way we thought about consuming music. It was the Model-T of our generation—an affordable device that changed our understanding of a concept in an instant.

Today, 1,000 songs in a hand-held device sounds like a joke. Additionally, this iPod had no touch screen, no color, no photos, no sound without headphones, and no way to make a phone call. Imagine that? What a piece of junk! It's a dinosaur of technology destined for a museum, if it's not already there, but there is a larger point to be made. This simple-looking device, while it pales in comparison to whatever latest technological advancement has come since, started it all. It did so precisely because it was and still is good design.

Before the first generation iPod, we listened to CDs, cassettes, vinyl, and before that, 8-track tapes. When Napster and Limewire first appeared, the idea of listening to music through a computer was revolutionary. When Mp3 players began appearing, it was amazing and exciting. Nevertheless, none gathered enough steam to take over the world and change minds. Then, came the iPod.

By 2004, the iPod had become a part of daily life for millions of users, including musicians and celebrities who were amazed with how simple it was to use. The layout *"reminds the musician of music,"* said John Mayer. Will Smith told Jay Leno and Wired magazine about his infatuation with *"the gadget of the century."* Gwyneth Paltrow confided her iPod-love to Vogue (her baby is named Apple — coincidence?) — http://www.newsweek.com/ipod-nation-130863

Sure, the iPod had its share of issues: battery life was a joke and replacing it was next to impossible. Apple's customer support was also extremely difficult to deal with during those rare times when you actually had to call. Nevertheless, the iPod presented a unique design of unmatched simplicity. Any of the annoyances were minor compared to the payoff, which was ease of use, the *cool* factor, portability, and a lot of music in your pocket. To get going, all you needed were some songs in the MP3 format and headphones. No directions/instructions needed. Now, of course, Apple could have turned this device into something more than just a music player. They could have included a radio, a to-do list application, or features similar to a palm pilot (remember those?). But they didn't. Why? Because Apple stayed focused on the problem at hand. With the introduction and popularity of digital music and Apple's previous innovation with iTunes, taking music with you was the next logical step. Sure, there were other devices out there, but none did it as *well* as Apple.

> *"From early on we wanted a product that would seem so natural and so inevitable and so simple you almost wouldn't think of it as having been designed."*
>
> *— Apple's industrial designer Ive,* http://www.newsweek.com/ipod-nation-130863

Good design isn't always original

Take a look at this image and tell me what you see. Does it look familiar?

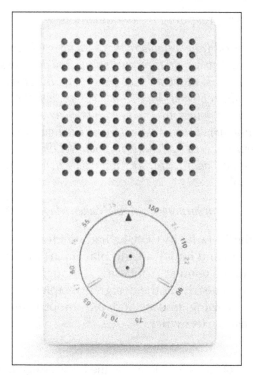

Source: https://www.pinterest.com/pin/510103095265024925/

This is a pocket radio, the model T3, designed by Dieter Rams in 1958. When asked what Rams thought about Apple products and what a Rams-designed computer might look like today, he said this:

> *"It would look like one of Apple's products. In many magazines, or on the Internet, people compare Apple products to things which I designed…I think their designs are brilliant. I don't consider it an imitation. I take it as a compliment."*

> *– Gary Hustwit, Dieter Rams: If I Could Do It Again, I Would Not Want To Be A Designer,* fastcomany.com.

The first generation iPod solved a unique and singular problem. But how was it innovative? Can design be innovative if we borrow designs from the past? Is this a principle of "good" design? Is this even creative?

This is, perhaps, my favorite response to that question:

> *"Nothing is original. Steal from anywhere that resonates with inspiration or fuels your imagination. Devour old films, new films, music, books, paintings, photographs, poems, dreams, random conversations, architecture, bridges, street signs, trees, clouds, bodies of water, light and shadows. Select only things to steal from that speak directly to your soul. If you do this, your work (and theft) will be authentic. Authenticity is invaluable; originality is non-existent. And don't bother concealing your thievery - celebrate it if you feel like it. In any case, always remember what Jean-Luc Godard said: 'It's not where you take things from - it's where you take them to'"*

> *– Jim Jarmusch, MovieMaker Magazine #53, January, 2004*

When Rams designed the T3 radio in 1958, he had no idea how much influence it would have on later design and how it would play a part in changing how we view the world. Steve Jobs and the team at Apple saw it though. This design and the iPod also take into consideration nearly all the design principles in one shot—innovation, usefulness, aesthetically pleasing, understandable, unobtrusive, honest, minimalist, and very valuable, at least for its owner.

The principle of h*onesty,* as Rams defined it, is design that does not make a product appear more innovative, powerful, or valuable than it really is. It does not attempt to manipulate the consumer with promises that cannot be kept.

– Dieter Rams 10 Principles of Good Design

Explore more Dieter Rams designs at
https://www.pinterest.com/dclaassens/dieter-rams/

Useful

For those too young to remember, there was a time when watching a favorite television show meant remembering to be in front of the TV at a certain time. Back then, you had one chance and if you missed it, well, you could call the TV station to send you a copy. Eventually, VHS made it possible to record TV. Cable television introduced multiple viewings and today, anything and everything can be seen within 30 seconds of thinking about it and available for unlimited viewings. It has gotten to the point where if something cannot be found between 4-30 seconds, it's simply not there. While many of us take this kind of thing for granted nowadays, having the world at our fingertips is quite amazing and still quite new. When it's done well, it is also extremely useful. YouTube provides a great example.

Even in its first incarnation, YouTube never required a lot of thought to figure it out. The search engine was always front and center, and the results were always highly satisfying, from videos one hoped to find to many wonderful surprises.

Since its inception and in the years that followed, not much has really changed. Here is YouTube in 2008:

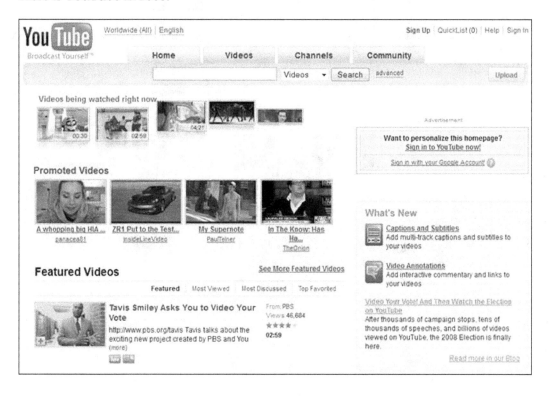

This is YouTube in 2012:

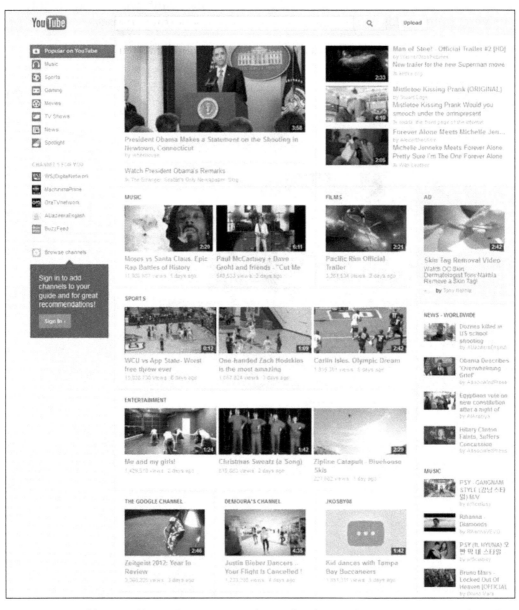

Source: http://newmediarockstars.com/2013/02/youtube-grows-up-a-visual-history-of-how-the-video-sharing-site-has-changed-over-the-past-8-years/

Visit YouTube today, and while there have been many enhancements, most of them are feature based, not really design based. In an 8-year period, YouTube's design and its information architecture, which we will talk about in the next chapter, have hardly changed. This is quality design, the kind we, as UX designers, should be striving for. YouTube got it right the first time and continues to dominate. It has become synonymous with online video, much like how Google is synonymous with search and the iPhone with mobile technology. If they do not define good design, then nothing does.

When you use good design, pay attention to it. Understand why it is good. Review the principles and find them in your favorite apps, websites, and anywhere else where your interaction is seamless and virtually invisible.

Minimalist

When we talk about good design, it doesn't only apply to devices and websites. It also applies to everything else, including software applications. A great example of this is Balsamiq, an application designed to build wireframes. It takes a similar approach to the iPod in its simplicity and singular focus.

 Incidentally, I wrote a book on Balsamiq called *The Balsamiq Wireframes Quickstart Guide*, which you can purchase from the same publisher (*Packt Publishing*) as this book.

Balsamiq is simple. Launch the application, and within minutes, your app is up and running. Here is a screen capture of some of Balsamiq's tools:

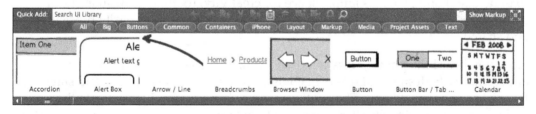

As you can see, the tool bar is very straightforward. It uses language familiar to designers and provides easy identification and understandability using visual elements. Below the tool bar is the canvas, where the tools and design elements can be dragged from the tool bar and manipulated.

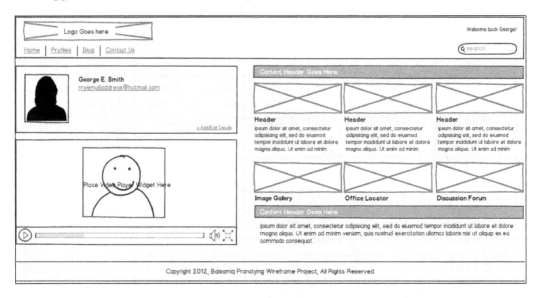

Balsamiq does a great job of avoiding the bells and whistles of busier, more complicated wireframing type tools such as Axure and Photoshop, which do much more than just wireframes. They are great tools, but Balsamiq is unique because it provides only the tools and menus needed for the task. It is also very simple to understand and provides ample space for creativity, room to grow in terms of features and add-ons, and allows for the expression of ideas to be easily presented and shared.

Have you heard the phrase, "less is more?" Well, as clichéd as it may sound, it applies nicely to design that does not confuse or distract, but simplifies and stays focused on the task at hand. The goal is to add only what provides value to the user and remove everything else. Knowing what not to include, however, is much harder to do. Before you make such decisions, know your audience, test your designs with them, and then, validate your findings and make improvements as needed.

Understandable

When we think of UX, a word that often comes to mind is "understandability," which, for UX design, has two distinct meanings:

- **How** to use an interface
- **Why** to use it

When a design fails at one or both of these, it can lead to significant problems. Let's look at an example. In 2015, *The New York Times* reported that Twitter, the online social networking service, was facing a problem:

> *"Top executives acknowledged…that despite huge name recognition for its social network, the vast majority of potential customers did not understand how or why to use the service, stunting its growth."*

> — http://www.nytimes.com/2015/07/29/technology/
> twitter-quarterly-earnings.html

With a user base of over 300 million, one would think Twitter was well past this type of problem. However, while Twitter is well-designed aesthetically and quite easy to use, it is still a difficult concept for many people to comprehend. To describe Twitter to a new user might go something like this: Twitter is a website where total strangers type short sentences into a text field and share them with their followers. When you read a tweet you can like, reply, or share it with your followers or with others using hashtags. Before long, you may get new followers who, if they like what you have to say, will follow you and you can then grow your social network. Get it?

For many people, this may be a clear and simple explanation. For others, it may elicit a response such as "Huh? Why would anyone use such a thing? What purpose does it serve? I don't get it!" Twitter also has another problem. Many of its board of directors do not Tweet! Also, the company has reportedly stopped disclosing the percentage of users who take no discernable user action, making it harder for investors to figure out whether Twitter's core user base is growing or dying. *– Twitter just made it harder to figure out how many inactive users it has,* businessinsider.com, *May, 2015.*

Understandable – how?

To understand good design in light of these problems, let's start with the "how" of good design. As web applications go, Twitter is easy to use. The design is also pretty minimalist and sticks to doing one thing pretty well. Usability on the site is also quite simple—a testament to the many millions of people who have signed up and use the site on a daily basis.

Essentially, this is all Twitter really is—a text field with a few basic tools and a **Tweet** button:

As you type, a text counter counts down the number of characters (**140** in all) and provides a visual indicator if you exceed that number. The user then clicks on the **Tweet** button and their tweet is posted for all your followers to behold. Users can also insert an image, create a poll, and interact with a number of other easy-to-use, useful features to help build a following and a social network.

It is in this next step where the magic or the mystery begins. For many people, after you submit a tweet, there is no immediate payoff. You might be staring at your comment wondering, "What now? How do I get followers? Is anyone reading this? Is anyone out there at all?" For many people, Twitter can seem like talking to an empty room or to a room full of people who are all talking at the same time, which brings us to the next aspect of understandability.

Understandable—why?

When we design, we often consider the "how" more than the "why." Twitter again provides a good example of this. A review of Twitter's registration application, filed with the **Securities and Exchange Commission (SEC)** in 2013, shows that Twitter was concerned about the "why" of their design. For example, in the section of the application titled Risk Factors, the company stated:

> *"A number of consumer-oriented websites that achieved early popularity have since seen their user bases or levels of engagement decline, in some cases precipitously. There is no guarantee that we will not experience a similar erosion of our user base or engagement levels. A number of factors could potentially negatively affect user growth and engagement."*

They go on to list a number of risk factors, including two that are most relevant:

> *"We are unable to convince potential new users of the value and usefulness of our products and services."*

> *"We are unable to present users with content that is interesting, useful and relevant to them."*

They conclude with this statement:

> *"If we are unable to increase our user growth or engagement, or if they decline, this could result in our products and services being less attractive to potential new users, as well as advertisers, which would have a material and adverse impact on our business, financial condition and operating results."*

If issues like this are key to Twitter's continued success, then having 300 million users means nothing unless the majority of them are active and engaged. — `http://www.sec.gov/Archives/edgar/data/1418091/000119312513390321/` `d564001ds1.htm#toc564001_4`. While the designs you are delivering may not affect the same number of customers/users as Twitter, the same principles apply. Make sure that your designs can clearly identify not only *how* to use it, but also be able to clearly and easily articulate *why* your customers/users want to use it. Base this not on your opinions or feelings, but on actual research over time to see whether your hypothesis bears this out or not. If not, it doesn't mean you need to scrap the idea — Twitter is very successful and a cultural phenomenon. However, keep in mind the problems you might face later and think about how you will address them.

Design using the three-second rule

There is a saying that originated in politics. It states, "If you're explaining, you're losing." Ironically, this also holds true for stand-up comedians, and it also qualifies for UX design. This does not mean UX, politics and stand-up comedy are alike, but similarly, with attention spans rapidly declining, it is more important than ever to engage and connect with our customers/users quickly, efficiently, effectively and to their satisfaction. This is not a new idea, but it should still be high on your list of priorities as a designer. Here's an example:

This is what Twitter looks like to the uninitiated, and before logging in.

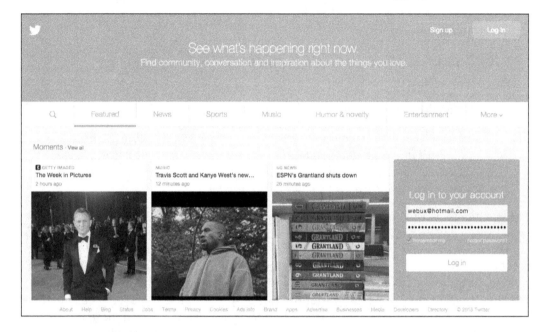

Can you immediately tell what kind of site this is? The header says, **Find community, conversation and inspiration about the things you love**. Hmmm…ok, maybe it's a community of some kind, but what kind? Am I supposed to know? I feel old. I'll just sign up and see what this is all about.

It is probably safe to assume that Twitter has millions of accounts with tweets similar to this one:

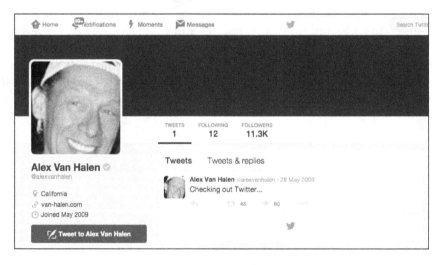

If you missed it, the preceding image shows a single tweet from 2009, followed by…nothing. Not a peep or tweet for 6 years. I think it is safe to assume that 11.3k followers are waiting patiently for tweet number two. Alex? Are you out there?

Designing applications that are easy is an accomplishment and what we strive for as UX designers, but if our customers/users don't understand what we give them or don't want it, then maybe it's time to reconsider. Imagine if Ford delivered the Model-T and people truly *did* love their horses more? Imagine if manure, flies, horse-related accidents, and fatalities were a non-issue? If so, why would people want an automobile? Perhaps, some might, but not in the numbers that Ford actually sold them. What if people truly loved reading maps while driving a car and would rather pull over in order to read printed directions from MapQuest or their highlighted paper map from AAA? (Yes, this is how it used to be.) What if GPS was a novelty, much like laser discs or the beta max? (Look it up.) How would you get people to change their behavior if they really didn't want to or didn't understand why they should?

Of course, these are absurd examples, because we all know about the problems they solved. However, the point is that solutions only work if we have an agreement from our customers/users that a problem exists. Then, it is our job to make sure we address the *how* and *why* of our solutions through testing and validation to make sure our users agree. It is always more practical and economical to learn this early rather than seeing our designs used one time and never again. When you have 300 million registered users, you can fix this over time, but the rest of us will not have such luxuries. Nevertheless, Twitter proved that even a cultural phenomenon experiences many of the same problems that come when understandability is not fully addressed. Time will tell how and if they can solve it.

Understandability – fail!

Here is an example of another design that tried but failed to get understandability under control. When mobile technology was really starting to ramp up, designers tried many ways to get users engaged to the point of relying on their mobile devices. One concept that tried but ultimately failed was QR codes. At one time, QR codes seemed to be everywhere, a way to facilitate a seemingly personalized digital interaction experience that was quick and easy. For many people, however, QR codes were confusing, both in terms of how to engage with them and their intrinsic value. One writer referred to QR codes as the blinking VCR clock of the 21st century.

"We all have the notion that a QR code contains information, a link perhaps that can be used on the Internet to gain access to even more information. But knowing what it is used for does not mean you know how to use it…how to scan it…or even create them."

— https://gigaom.com/2015/01/31/why-qr-codes-are-the-blinking-vcr-clock-of-the-21st-century/

Source:http://www.qrstuff.com/images/sample.png

To make matters worse, when users interacted with QR codes, they were often taken to useless sites that were not optimized for mobile or that led to broken or irrelevant links. Many other pages had no clear call to action. Of course, when QR codes *did* work, it was primarily due to the designer's creativity. For example, some provided links to free music downloads while other allowed users to pay for an item and have it shipped, and so on. — http://www.sentrymarketing.com/2015/03/qr-codes-the-final-wordprobably/. Nevertheless, much of it turned out to be too little too late for QR codes. Don't let the same thing happen to your designs. Test, validate, make it understandable, make it valuable, and then deliver.

Valuable

As mentioned earlier, this characteristic was not on Rams' original list. However, for a UX designer, it is an important principle to follow, if not the most important of all.

Think about some of your favorite apps and devices, and how they have benefitted you and improved your life, even if only a little. The Internet itself provides value. It aided in most of the research for this book. Most of the websites you frequent are valuable too, at least for you. In this regard, value can also be subjective. For UX designers, value means identifying the reason why a customer/user would want to engage with your design and then providing something in return for their time. Even if the payoff is not immediate, perhaps, it promises to be so sometime in the future. For example, leaving comments on Amazon could turn you into a top reviewer or land you a spot in their customer-reviewer *hall of fame.*

LinkedIn can increase your professional network, allowing access to important connections and, maybe, even land you a job. Post a funny video on YouTube, and before you know it, the video goes viral and you are famous! Sign on to a dating website, and Mr. or Ms. Right may be a click away.

Understandability is one thing, but giving your customers/users an immediate feeling that your design may benefit them in some way is just as valuable and something to aim for in your work. Facebook, LinkedIn, Twitter, YouTube, Amazon, GPS, dating sites, all provide a return on the user's investment of time. They also provide tremendous value in terms of user interest, interaction, engagement, and value. We will talk more about this later. For now, ask yourself these important questions:

- What value does your design solution provide to your customers/users?

- How will your design solution improve their lives?

- Why should your customers/users bother engaging with your solution? What proof do you have that they really want to? Have you asked? Have you done any research to find out?

- What problem are you solving, and what will improve as a result?

- Why should anyone care about your solution? What's in it for them?

- What are some scenarios that demonstrate how/why your design solution provides value?

- How will you know if it does? What metrics are you going to capture and track to find out?

These are all important questions to ask yourself and your team. Do not settle for less than very compelling answers. Try them out on your next project and see how easy or difficult it is to get answers and information that you can use to improve your designs.

Safety

What comes to mind when you think of safe design? Perhaps the location and signage of building exists? The automatic cutoff button on heavy machinery? Traffic signals and circuit breakers? Maybe the location of the fuel selector valve on a do-it-yourself airplane? Certainly, these are all important considerations that can save lives, but what does safety mean for your work?

Actually, Rams referred to this principle as environmentally friendly design—*design that makes an important contribution to the preservation of the environment.* — `https:// www.quora.com/Will-the-ten-principles-of-good-design-by-Dieter- Rams-be-obsolete-any-time-in-the-future`. In the world of interactive online experiences, environmental friendliness is hard to qualify. Therefore, I've replaced it with *Safety,* a close relative in terms of good UX design. Let's look at an example.

Today, mobile devices are the dominant form of online engagement. At last count, there are more mobile devices than people in the world. —`http://www. independent.co.uk/life-style/gadgets-and-tech/news/there-are- officially-more-mobile-devices-than-people-in-the-world-9780518. html`. That's astounding, and a bit disturbing. Nevertheless, it also means that as UX designers, we have to approach design from an entirely new perspective, one that accounts for *where* our customers are when they are interacting with our design solutions. Before technology went mobile, UX practitioners designed with a user's location in mind, but normally, this meant their desk. It was stationary, and for the most part, so were they. Today, users are everywhere and doing almost everything while using their mobile devices. As a result, safety has become a top concern and a high priority, or at least, it should be.

For example, GPS technology was designed specifically for use while driving. One app that handles GPS well is called Waze. It not only provides excellent directions, it also alerts drivers to vehicles stopped at the side of the road, accidents, police presence, traffic jams, and even road kill. Waze, like all GPS apps, does a great job with voice too, alerting drivers very audibly to what's coming down the road while allowing them to keep their eyes on the road instead of on a small screen. While this is great for an app *intended* for use while driving, what about the apps that aren't?

Mobile phones are banned while driving in many states, and nearly all ban texting while behind the wheel. Let's be honest though, does this mean we are going to comply? For a UX designer to ignore this reality would be irresponsible, naïve, and downright dangerous. If we are truly going to think about safety, then we must consider all situations, regardless of the law or common sense.

An example of an application with safety in mind is Voice Memos, an app designed for those times when a pen is nowhere in sight and when a thought or idea just needs to be captured. Now, I want to make it clear that I am not condoning using an app like Voice Memos while driving; anyone using it should not be driving or at least pulled over before considering it, but let's be real for a moment. Is it our job as UX designers to design for how we *want* people to use our solutions, or do we also need to consider other alternatives? That's a rhetorical question, but it deserves an answer nevertheless. As UX designers, we simply cannot ignore the alternative. We are not doing our job if we do.

Voice Memos is an app that comes already installed on an iPhone, and it's a fine choice for what it does. With this app in mind, let's consider a scenario, It's nighttime. You're driving down the highway on your way home from work. It's been a long day and you and your team spent hours working through a design problem and went nowhere. As you round the curve, a great idea suddenly pops into your head. You've solved the problem! You realize that it has to be captured or you will forget it. You search in the darkness for a pen. Nothing. You consider stopping at a gas station, but the next exit is still a few miles away, and you are already running late for dinner. Do you chance losing the thought, or do you grab your phone and open an app like Voice Memos?

One more time, I want to make clear that driving and using one's phone is a bad idea. It may even be illegal where you are. If you have to use your phone, for goodness' sake, pull over! At the same time, we cannot talk about safety in design and ignore the fact that people will do it anyway. To ignore this fact is to ignore reality and the safety of our customers and users.

Provide affordances

While launching Voice Memos, the first thing you'll see is a big red button against a black background. This is a great example of affordance—a UX term meaning design that quickly suggests *how the object should be used, a visual clue to its function and use.* The first thing to notice is the red record button. Even if you are color blind, this design still provides a very clear indication that there is something to press to start recording.

Even if the user still doesn't get it, there is nothing else to do on the screen, and since the only purpose for this app is to record, there *should* be only one thing to do. — `https://www.interaction-design.org/literature/book/the-glossary-of-human-computer-interaction/affordances`.

Source: `http://uxarchive.com/apps/voice`

Even while driving, which I am not condoning, the user can easily see the record button against the black background and know what to do with just the slightest glance. As the app begins recording, a vertical indicator slides across the screen, showing a graphical representation of your voice or whatever sound source you may be capturing. The app has other information too, but all we care about is that it's doing what we expect it to do.

Stopping the recording is just as easy. Simply tap the large red button again, only now it's at the bottom of the screen. Notice how the shape changed too. In this case, one click stops the recording. Now, I wouldn't recommend doing anything further while driving, such as saving the file, naming it, or editing it. All you really care about anyway is that you recorded the memo. You can deal with the other details later when you get home.

Source: http://uxarchive.com/apps/voice

Long-lasting design

The final design principle that we will talk about in this chapter is long-lasting design or design that maintains its *conceptual integrity* over time. In the realm of UX, long-lasting design begins and ends with a solid foundation, one whose original intent, understanding, familiarity, and usefulness remain intact even as additional features are added over time. Long-lasting design is a solution that can grow and change over time, without the need to tear the underlying structure apart to do it. Long-lasting design is one that works like a system, where all elements of the design are working together to support each other. Another term for this is *conceptual integrity*, or a term that may be more familiar: **Information Architecture**, something we will look at in detail in the next chapter.

> *Conceptual integrity is THE most important consideration. A consistent deficient system is arguably 'better' than one that contains many good but independent and uncoordinated ideas.*
>
> *– Frederick P. Brooks Jr., The Mythical Man-Month: Essays on Software Engineering.*

We live in a world where iPhones are outdated in a year and a car's computer system can be updated overnight; 60,000 Tesla owners discovered this when they woke up to find their car's computer system had been updated with hands-free driving functionality. — `http://qz.com/538436/tesla-model-s-autopilot/`. While good design provides for "here" and "now" it is more importantly designed for "later". Good design can grow, improve, expand and evolve along with business, customer and user needs.

Design exercise

Take some time to review the remaining design principles:

- aesthetically pleasing
- unobtrusive
- honest
- thorough

Now, find examples of each. Do any of the examples we already discussed qualify? Are there others? Use this opportunity to engage your classmates, your colleagues, your business partners, and your development team in this conversation and see how many you can come up with together. It's a great opportunity to start speaking the same language of design.

To learn more about Dieter Rams and to see his Ten Principles in action using his earlier design work as reference, visit `https://www.vitsoe.com/us/about/good-design`.

Native advertising revisited

If you recall the example of *native advertising* from earlier in this chapter, I said we would return to it later. So, after reviewing the *ten principles for good design*, what is the verdict? Is native advertising a good design? Is native advertising subjective? Is it innovative? Is it useful? Is it minimalist? Is it understandable? Is it valuable? It is safe, long lasting, aesthetically pleasing, unobtrusive, honest, and thorough? Perhaps, some of these qualify, but certainly not all. Does it matter? Does good design have to adhere to all of them? These are great questions to ponder. Take the time to do so. Your customers/users will be grateful that you did.

Summary

In this chapter, we explored the concept of "good" design, presented and explored the ten principles of good design and learned by example how these principles help to identify and create good design. Becoming a UX leader means being able to identify and create good design in your own work. Learning from great designers and designs it one of the best ways to do this. As you will see in the next chapter and in Chapter 5, *Patterns, Properties and Principles of Good UX Design*, good design is often achieved by looking at it from a much wider perspective.

Keep these principles close by. Copy them down, print them out, and remember them. Look for examples of them in your favorite apps, websites, applications, and in your everyday life and work. Good design is everywhere. It is literally all around you. Take notice!

4
Foundations of Good IA

One of the often overlooked and undervalued skills of the UX practitioner is Information Architecture, or IA. IA is to content and functionality what wireframes are to visual design. IA is the skeleton that informs visual design and dictates what information the user will see and interact with. IA is how information is organized and prioritized, and IA helps customers/users navigate through their experience.

In this chapter, we will:

- Focus on the fundamentals of IA to better understand how good IA guides customers/users to a desired outcome.

- Introduce **The Four Cs of IA**—a checklist of sorts to help validate your IA work.

- Learn from example the presence of IA in our everyday lives and how that translates online to inform and improve UX design.

Recognizing IA as an important aspect of your work as a UX practitioner and understanding how and why it works will improve your user's experience and the quality and success of your UX design work.

Foundational IA

It's impossible to talk about UX and technology and not talk about IA, but if we talk about it only from a technology this perspective, we create a very narrow understanding of it. For example, here is how Wikipedia defines IA:

> **Information architecture (IA)** *is the structural design of shared information environments; the art and science of organizing and labeling websites, intranets, online communities and software to support usability and findability; and an emerging community of practice focused on bringing principles of design and architecture to the digital landscape.*

While this definition is accurate in terms of technology, it is not the whole picture. When you expand this definition, you find that IA has been around much longer. In fact, a more accurate definition of IA comes not from technology, but from architecture (the kind that builds buildings). Here is a quote from an influential architect and the founder of TED talks, Richard Saul Wurman:

> *"I use the word information in its truest sense. Most of the word information contains the word inform, so I call things information only if they inform me, not if they are just collections of data, of stuff."*

As Wurman implied, we can organize piles of information all day long, but this doesn't necessarily inform us about anything, and it doesn't automatically create good IA. Information becomes useful only when it provides a foundation on which learning can take place. For example, the next time you are in a supermarket, notice how everything is organized and arranged. What you're seeing is the result of carefully constructed IA right in front of your eyes.

Supermarket IA is designed to make you spend more time and money in the store — much like how casinos are designed without clocks in order to make you forget about the world outside for a while and totally immerse yourself in the experience. Good IA is designed to immerse us in an experience and guide us seamlessly through it without discomfort, while perhaps providing some learning and discovery along the way. IA, both good and bad, affects our mood, thoughts, and behavior. To do this effectively, IA requires focus in many areas. To ensure this happens, it is important to focus our efforts on four important areas, and what I call **The Four Cs of IA**.

The Four Cs of IA

When you first enter a supermarket, at least in the U.S., you will often encounter sights, sounds, and smells designed to grab your attention and keep you engaged for the duration of your shopping experience. Often, one of the first items you will encounter are fresh flowers — strategically placed to create a pleasant scent and a feeling of freshness as you walk in. Next, you may smell fresh baked bread or rotisserie chicken. Those are meant to overwhelm your senses and make you think about food, thus adding more to your cart as you shop. Perhaps you are already salivating as you read this. If so, you're not alone:

> *"We know those smells get your salivary glands working. When you're salivating, you're a much less disciplined shopper."*
>
> – *50 Supermarket Tricks You Still Fall For, Reader's Digest Magazine, February 2014*

Fruits and vegetables usually come next, presenting their bright colors, along with special lighting designed to brighten your mood and give the impression that everything was picked that day. It wasn't, of course. It actually came from a box in the back freezer, but if we knew that, we might not find it as appealing. Some produce departments even go so far as to spray their vegetables with a fine mist of water as the refrain from *Singin' in the Rain* plays in the background. It's a nice touch that really drives the point of freshness home.

Source: http://www.corriganmist.com/wp-content/uploads/ultramist-spray.jpg

"The place is fresh, the place is good. [Now we can] begin the journey. – A Few More Ways That Supermarkets Mess With Your Mind, businessinsider.com.*"*

Before you know it, you are fully immersed and engaged in a well-coordinated shopping experience, purposely designed to engage the senses quickly, efficiently, and quite effectively. Let's look at the four Cs of IA and see how they come into play:

- **Coordination**: The supermarket experience presents thousands of products and choices coordinated in a way that allows customers/users to process it all very quickly. Without this coordination, it's possible to become overwhelmed and confused about what to do first. Therefore, coordinating information allows for a clear starting and end point as well as guidance along the way. Think of IA as an ecosystem of information, where one piece of information connects to another using visual cues, sights, sounds, content, navigation, and so on, providing the customer/user with a kind of sensory map that guides them successfully to their ultimate destination.

- **Cooperation**: As we make our way through the shopping experience, we will come across many distractions. Distractions are a normal part of the IA experience and are not only unavoidable, but we actually seek them out! How easily and quickly we can recover from these distractions and still reach our ultimate goal will determine how cooperative the IA we are interacting with really is.

- **Change**: Good IA is designed to move customer/users through an experience quickly and efficiently. It also allows for change to occur without the need for refactoring the underlying structure of the design. Returning to the supermarket example, this could mean different products being showcased, new items being added to the shelves, and so on. The IA doesn't change though because its the underlying framework, providing the means for change to take place seamlessly. Similar IA exists online as well, with websites such as Amazon, Facebook, and CNN, where content changes quickly, although the experience stays the same.

- **Consequence**: The last of the four Cs is "consequence," meaning user outcomes versus user experience versus outlay of time and resources to reach the intended goal. For a business stakeholder, the consequences are measurable improvements, profits, **return on investment (ROI)**, new customers, higher customer satisfaction ratings, and so on. For a customer/user, it might mean a quick and painless interaction or an enjoyable one where the information and objectives they sought were met appropriately and to their expectations.

The Four Cs of IA are important criteria that act as a kind of checklist for all future IA improvements. Information that is coordinated, cooperative, open to change, and that results in consequences that benefit everyone involved is what we are striving for. We will look at the four Cs as they appear in examples throughout this chapter.

Navigation

Take a look at the following image. Does it remind you of anything? Perhaps navigation on a website?

Source: https://c1.staticflickr.com/7/6181/6060679268_073789ebf6_b.jpg

It's possible that the design of this bakery sign was intended to mimic website navigation, but more to the point, it demonstrates that navigation is required regardless of the medium within which it is presented. The sign in this image can also be easily seen from just about anywhere in the store. Navigation like this could be used in an online setting as well. Getting around, knowing where we are at any point in the process, and finding our way to an objective easily is what IA is all about.

Mental models

Here is another example of a supermarket:

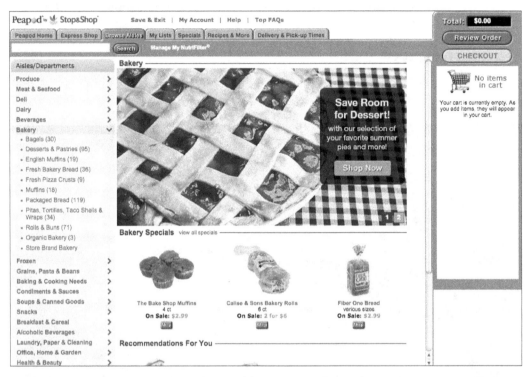

Source: http://www.peapod.com/

Although you can't smell the flowers or the rotisserie chicken in the preceding image, this virtual supermarket is no doubt designed according to specific customer expectations, what practitioners call **mental models**. Mental models help designers understand how customers/users think about how something should work based on their past experiences in similar situations. Without knowing the users mental model, we are simply guessing and making assumptions about what we *think* our users want. This is "faster horses" thinking and something we want to avoid at all costs. There is no substitute for research, observation, and testing of our solutions with real users, regardless of how certain we may feel about our work. Remember that the risk of being wrong is far greater than the time it takes to make sure we are right.

Taxonomy

Once we know our user's mental models, the next step is to organize that information using a component of IA called "taxonomy." Taxonomy is the method used to group, label, prioritize, and tag information to allow for greater findability, readability, and overall usability of the information being presented.

In the following image of a sitemap for an online college library, we can see an example of how taxonomy can be used:

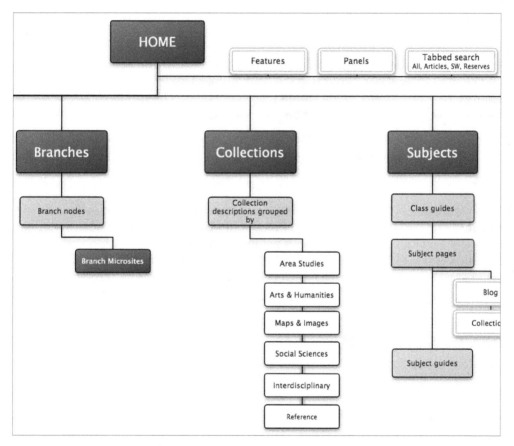

Source: https://lib.stanford.edu/files/sitemap-v2.2.jpg

Sitemaps

A sitemap is literally a visual map of information detailing the various paths we want our customers/users to take. The main objective of a sitemap is to create a hierarchy and a schema for how information will be coordinated, how it will cooperate, how it can change, and the consequences of this once it becomes a functioning, visual design.

Sitemaps are also very useful when you begin creating wireframes and prototypes, since you will have already worked through many of the potential obstacles that could have derailed later.

Looking again at the sitemap image, notice how the information is organized. There are top-level sections, such as **Branches**, **Collections**, and **Subjects** as well as subsections beneath them, providing the content that will be presented within them. All of this, of course, leads to the **Home** page, which branches off to some additional sections — **Features**, **Panels**, and **Tabbed Search** — as well.

 Some applications used for building detailed sitemaps include Microsoft Visio and Omnigraffle.

As you can see in the preceding image, IA and taxonomy provide a way to not only map out the flow of information, but to map it out based on the user's mental model. A library is something we can all recall visiting in person, and thus, we expect the online version to be organized in a similar way. Of course, not every website functions in the same way. As a result, it is important to know about the variety of taxonomies available.

Taxonomy types

There are four main taxonomy types to be aware of:

- Flat
- Hierarchical
- Faceted
- Networked

It's also important to note that different taxonomies are not mutually exclusive and can work very well when used together. Let's discuss the taxonomies one by one:

- **Flat taxonomy**: This is essentially a top-level list with no subcategories. For example, if you were designing a supermarket website, this could be a top level list of all the fruits and vegetables in the produce section.

- **Hierarchical taxonomy**: This is an organizational structure based on a hierarchical relationship (**Parent/Child**). For example, in the following example from `zappos.com`, the navigation shown is organized with high-level categories - **Shoes, Clothing, Bags & Handbags** as (**Parent**) and lower level ones - **WOMEN'S SHOES, MEN'S SHOES**, and so on, as (**Child**).

Shoes	Clothing	Bags & Handbags	Accessories	Watches	Boutiques	Wome

WOMEN'S SHOES	MEN'S SHOES	GIRLS' SHOES	BOYS' SHOES
Casual Shoes	Casual Shoes	Boots	Boots
Dress Shoes	Dress Shoes	Sneakers	Sneakers
Athletic Shoes	Athletic Shoes	Flats	Sandals
Work Shoes	Work Shoes	Sandals	Oxfords
Career Shoes	Career Shoes	Slippers	Slippers
Heels	Sneakers	Infant	Infant
Boots	Boots	Toddler	Toddler
Flats	Loafers	Youth	Youth
Sandals	Sandals	New Arrivals	New Arrivals
Slippers	Oxfords	View all...	View all...
Sneakers	Boat Shoes		
Wedges	Slippers		
Platforms	New Arrivals		
New Arrivals	View all...		
View all...			

Source: `zappos.com`

Alphabetized lists also use hierarchical taxonomy, as shown in this example of Amazon's search menu:

Source: Amazon.com

- **Faceted taxonomy**: This is an organizational structure where information can be sorted and filtered in multiple ways. Here, there is no specific hierarchy because of the need for cross-referencing various types of data to create more focused results. For example, in the following image, we see a filtering menu for men's shoes. Each section allows for various filtering in order to finely tune the results:

Source: Zappos.com

- **Networked taxonomy**: This is an organizational structure that allows for the cross-referencing and sorting of information on demand. An example would be sorting and grouping information using various criteria, as shown here using the `Amazon.com` **sort by** functionality:

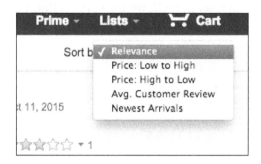

Source: `Amazon.com`

How you choose to organize information is the culmination of many factors, including knowing your customers/users, understanding their mental models, and using site maps and taxonomy. In addition, you will also want to consider how you are going to manage all this information once the site is ready to launch and thereafter. As a result, designing for change is an important consideration for good IA.

Designing for change

Of all the four Cs, perhaps the most important one is change. When we think about change, a question often arises about how it will affect our design. Will it require a complete rethinking, like when cameras went from film to digital? Will it mean making room in our current design for something new, like adding new products or new categories to an existing online store? What effect will change have on your taxonomy and your design? All these considerations are important to ensure that your well-designed IA remains that way long after you have created it.

Supermarkets are great at change. New products are added, while others are removed, and never are there disruptions to the overall experience or the layout of the store. Categories and aisles have been so well-placed and coordinated that there is really no need for change, despite products coming and going on a regular basis. Now, that's good IA.

We see this online as well with sites such as Amazon, Facebook, Pinterest, YouTube, CNN, and many others, all built for change. They change on a second-by-second basis without missing a beat. With good IA, changes are enhancements to what already exists, rather than new functionality to be relearned.

This applies to web and mobile applications too, such as GPS applications, which present constantly changing data and information requiring our attention, if you recall from the previous chapter, Waze is a a GPS application that makes getting to your destination enjoyable. From the moment Waze is opened, it provides a coordinated and cooperative experience that is hard to beat. It's an app that alerts drivers to all kinds of potential hazards and distractions, such as traffic, accidents, police presence, vehicles stopped on the side of the road, and and so on. All the while, Waze is working to guide us to our destination.

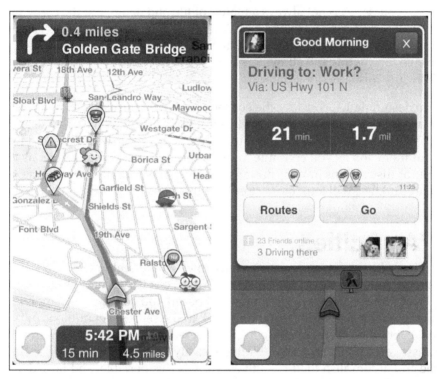

Source: http://media.idownloadblog.com/wp-content/uploads/2013/11/waze-ios-7-1024x846.png

Waze provides social features as well, such as how many Facebook friends are online and how many drivers using Waze are nearby. It also allows drivers to add to its database whatever road-related issues they encounter in order to alert other drivers following a similar route. In terms of change, Waze, like any GPS application, delivers new information so seamlessly that you won't notice anything has occurred unless, of course, you take a wrong turn. Otherwise, Waze quietly does its job, coordinating, cooperating, and changing, all with the consequence of delivering a safe, well-mapped route to your destination.

Change and consequences

Designing an application like Waze is serious business. Just the fact that Waze is used while driving is reason enough to consider the dangers. Now, add to that the potential for social interaction and alerting drivers to road hazards, and you've got IA that is not only constantly changing, but also creating multiple distractions that could figuratively and literally lead its users into a ditch.

With so much potential for distraction, good IA, as well as safety, is more important than ever. Of course, IA is not always a matter of life and death, but the consequences of poorly designed IA can feel just as real. Adding change to your designs is one thing, but if it can become potentially damaging, then it is vital that change occurs seamlessly and even enjoyably while still allowing the user to arrive on time at their destination and without any mishaps along the way.

As you are designing IA, consider the consequences of failure as well as success and plan accordingly. Remember to always test your solutions with real users, talk to them, observe them, and allow them to interact with your designs as you learn more about them and as you continue to make improvements. Remember as well to account for distractions in your designs, which can be equally challenging to navigate around. We will look more closely at this next.

The IA of cities

Imagine a busy city street, one where a newcomer would feel immediately overwhelmed, for example, Times Square in New York City. The sights, sounds, and smells of Times Square are extremely fast paced and constantly changing. Experiencing it for the first time can be a shock to the senses, yet millions of people navigate it every day, accomplishing millions of tasks in this frenetic environment. Even tourists can navigate the area relatively easily while still managing to have a good time and accomplish their objectives. How is this possible, and how does this relate to good design and good IA?

Source: `https://c1.staticflickr.com/5/4060/4235464424_7eeb083746_b.jpg`

Fractal loading

As cities grow more complex, city planners continue to study ways to improve them and our experiences within them. Planning for such complexities requires a deep understanding of people, cultures, and languages. It also requires the ability to inform as well as to allow for a multitude of objectives to be accomplished with minimum discomfort and confusion.

This same approach is also needed for website design, as it too works to make order out of chaos. To do this effectively requires careful coordination and cooperation of information so that even when we are bombarded with data, we are still able to understand the bigger picture and achieve our objectives. The scientific name for this kind of informational organization is fractal loading, or the coexistence of different, but related things at different levels of scale. — `http://zeta.math.utsa.edu/~yxk833/InfoCities.html`.

Fractal loading is important in IA because everything we design has to compete with many distractions, whether they are ones we've created or external ones. For example, consider your commute to work. Along the way, you will surely encounter distractions, some enjoyable and maybe some not so enjoyable. Some of these distractions may even provide value and learning unrelated to your main objective of getting to work. Perhaps you pass a new restaurant that you want to try or you stop at a store to purchase something for your home. Maybe you get a flat tire and stop to repair it. Amidst all of this, it is safe to assume that you didn't forget your main objective. You still remembered to go to work, find your desk, get some coffee, say hello to coworkers, and so on. The point is that throughout our day, we experience distractions and even seek them out. It is important to remember and to plan for this in our design work.

Now, I am not suggesting adding distractions to your designs just to have them. This would be counterintuitive. I am posing the question, however, that since distractions are unavoidable, how will you account for them in your designs when they occur?

Focused IA

Helping users to focus is just as important as helping them when they can't. As you plan for IA, consider the kinds of distractions that could occur and how to avoid them. For example, are you providing intuitive navigation? Are there mental models to consider that will keep your customers/users on track and focused? What do you want users to learn and/or discover along the way? Can objectives be completed easily, or will confusion and panic lead to calls to customer support or giving up in frustration? What happens when users veer off course? Can they easily find their way back? What if users are in a hurry and don't have time for diversions? Have you provided a clear path? Are you even aware if these issues exist? Have you planned and budgeted for usability studies to observe how users behave and respond to your design? Have you interviewed users to understand what they might need from your design? If you cannot answer these questions affirmatively and in detail or you are wondering why any of this is important, consider what happens when these questions are ignored.

Imagine driving down a dark road in an unfamiliar town during a snowstorm. You have no GPS, your phone battery died, and the charger is at home. On top of this, you car is nearly out of gas. In this potentially panicked state, your ability to take in new information is dramatically reduced. You may be focused on the objective of finding a gas station, but you are certainly not enjoying the experience or seeing any value in it. On the other hand, if you were driving a hybrid vehicle, you may have had an added bit of security and a feeling of safety because of its reserve battery. In other words, you can still run out of gas, and the car will reach its destination, allowing you to continue on your way without fail. If you find that your IA can potentially lead your customers/users down a dark road with no way out, don't panic and continue reading.

Food for thought

Before cities, humans were simple wanderers, hunters, and explorers. As our surroundings changed and our interactions grew more complex, we moved away from our natural tendencies and instincts to more unnatural ones. The fact is, though, that while the need for information and access to it has grown more complex, we still seek the same simplicity, ease of use, and a clear path. It is, therefore, our responsibility as designers to provide this in our work and to reconnect with our end user's instinctual needs. It is already being done, and the more we are able to notice it, the better we will be at delivering it. Let's take a closer look at how this is being accomplished in the digital realm.

Fractal loading on the web

If you are familiar with CNN, then you know that they provide a lot of information at breakneck speed. As millions of users consume that information, CNN has a created a very complex job for itself. A user coming to CNN has many objectives, primarily to get news and information. Sometimes, this may be for research purposes, sometimes to catch up on the day's events, and sometimes to know the sports scores from the previous night's games. In other words, CNN has a lot of diversions and distractions, yet it is still one of the top news sites on the Internet.

For example, at any given moment, CNN is changing. One moment their home page can look like this:

Source: cnn.com

And the next moment, it can look like this:

Source: cnn.com

It's the same home page, but it's been dramatically altered, primarily because something important and more newsworthy than the previous headline occurred — at least as far as CNN is concerned. What's worth noting, however, is that this altered design could be a major distraction and confusing to many people, especially if you don't care about politics. Nevertheless, CNN's designers provided an easy solution. By simply scrolling down the page, all the other stories are still there. In fact, if you look under the photos, you can still see some of them (look at the arrow in the following screenshot):

 In web design parlance, the technique of displaying information so that it can be seen without having to scroll is called **above the fold**, referring to the bottom of the users screen (the fold) and what appears above it. Good design requires important information to be viewable at first glance, without having to scroll and in order to avoid confusion. It may sound hard to believe, but failing to scroll is something that happens all the time. Never assume what your users will do and always make it clear what you want them to do.

Throughout the CNN experience, their designers have devised other clever solutions to potential user distractions. For example, pages that provide video allow the user to scroll and continue reading while the video shrinks and moves to the upper-right corner of the page, as shown in the following screenshot.

This allows for simultaneous viewing of both written and video formats. Whether you find this bit of technology useful or annoying, it is still a strong solution to a user issue that CNN felt was important enough to solve.

Source: cnn.com

As attention spans grow shorter and our appetite for information increases, what and how we design is more important than ever. Learning from those who do it well is important too. The amount of information available to us at any given time has the potential to create digital and physical noise that competes for our attention and can drown out what may be important to us. The fact that we are able to navigate through this noise and find what we want and need is a testament not only to our brain's ability to parse data, but also to good design and IA. As UX designers, the need for more and more information creates an ever challenging and unique opportunity, not only to do it better, but more importantly to do it well.

Gauging your IA success

Salvador Dalí once said, "Have no fear of perfection—you'll never reach it."

As defeating as this quote may sound, your objective as a UX practitioner is not to reach perfection, but to create design that is meaningful, understandable, useful, and engaging. To gauge your success in these areas, ask yourself these important questions:

- Is the information presented coordinated in such a way that it is quickly and easily understandable?

- It content presented and written at a level that your specific readers can understand?

- How great is the effort for users to cooperate with your design? Will they want to willingly or begrudgingly? Have you tested this with real users to know for sure?

- Is the right amount of information being presented? Too much information? Too little? Have you spent enough time editing the content and sharing it with potential users to make sure it is easily readable and understandable?

- Can content be edited to avoid numerous pages when a summary might be sufficient?

- Does the search functionality provide quality results? Can someone find exactly what he or she is looking for?

- Have you tested the search functionality with actual users, using various, real-world scenarios that range from simple to complex?

- Have you designed the IA to account for changes, whether planned or unplanned? Can you list some scenarios that would validate this? What plans do you have in place to address change when it is required?

- How easy is it to maintain the site and update it when needed?

- How often will change occur, and how quickly will updates need to be made?

- How much training will your customers/users need in order to learn how to use or navigate your design?

- What could be made simpler to avoid the need for training altogether?

- How much time does it take to accomplish the main objective of your design? Do you have a benchmark for how long it should take verses actual time?

- What distractions might occur during the user's interaction with your design that may detract from their experience? How have you accounted for this?

- What value might users gain from distraction within your design? What can they learn?

- What are the consequences for your customers/users if they fail to reach their objective quickly and easily? What about the consequences for you and your company?

To gauge IA success, prepare for the challenges, obstacles, and detours that lie in wait, even if you cannot yet see them. Test them with real users to find them and to overcome them in your designs. Plan early, anticipate, test, learn, and improve.

Maps

"Everything is a map of something"

– Richard Saul Wurman

As you read the next section, think about where you are right now, physically. Did you use a map to get there? Did you have to navigate any obstacles? Were there distractions? Did you make any new discoveries? Did you meet your objectives? Were your tasks easy to complete?

Everyday we are on a journey that requires thought, guidance, and guarantees that we will arrive successfully. It may not even be a physical journey. Writing this book was a journey, for example, with a very clear destination: You reading it! Most of our daily activities, such as shopping, commuting to work, and using our phones, are all fairly easy to accomplish now, but think back to something like learning to drive, starting a new job, learning an instrument, and so on. What you might now take for granted was new at one time and required guidance from an instructor, a colleague, a book, and a lot of practice. Maybe you took to these new tasks quickly, while others needed more time.

Good IA is something we often take for granted too. The reason is that good IA instructs and guides us without our being aware of it. This is accomplished using another important component of IA called Wayfinding.

Wayfinding

There are four basic characteristics of Wayfinding:

- Orientation
- Route decision
- Route monitoring
- Destination recognition

https://en.wikipedia.org/wiki/Wayfinding

Let's take a closer look, beginning with the next example:

Source: https://bccollege1.files.wordpress.com/2013/01/bellevue-
square-0401.jpg

Do you recognize the map in the preceding image? For anyone unfamiliar, it's a shopping mall map, and it provides all four of the characteristics of Wayfinding. This next image provides a better look:

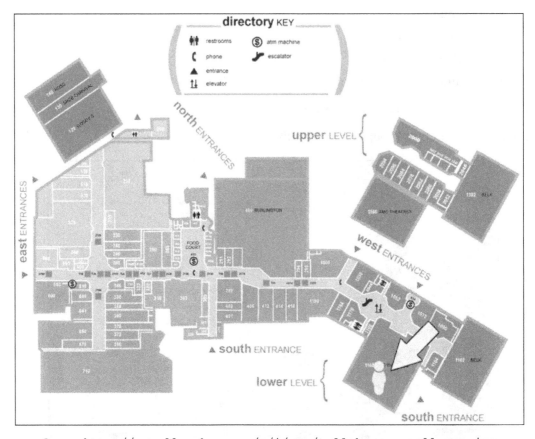

Source: `http://m.mallseeker.com/m/i/map/tallahassee-mall-map.jpg`

- **Orientation**: If you look closely at the preceding map, an arrow points to an icon of a person. The icon, added for example purposes, is used to provide orientation as we progress through the store. Providing users with orientation allows them to gauge their progress towards an objective and a destination, shows them how far they have come and the distance remaining, and what obstacles or distractions they might encounter along the way. In website design, this is often done using the Home button or a "Home" related icon in the upper-left corner of the screen. It is also accomplished in a number of other ways, such as using a stationary tool bar at the top of the screen that doesn't move when the user scrolls. It is not "how" that matters as much as it is making sure that the user always knows where they are throughout the experience.

- **Route decision**: Once the user has become oriented to their surroundings, they need to find the quickest, most direct route to get there. A mall map is easy because the user can see the whole picture at once. A website requires more careful consideration. If you recall the online library sitemap from earlier, here is a more complete version:

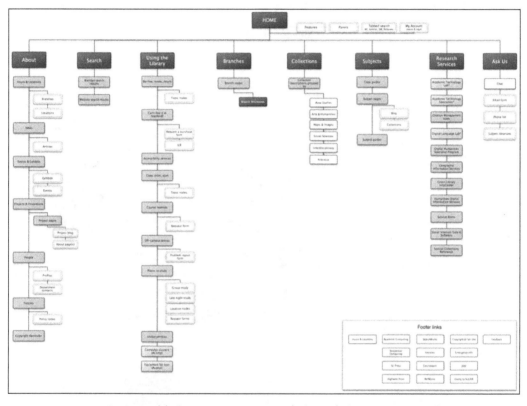

Source: `https://lib.stanford.edu/files/sitemap-v2.2.jpg`

Before you begin guiding your customers/users, you would want to know what the entire landscape looks like from a high level. Sitemaps provide a full view, allowing the designer to create coordinated and cooperative experiences that function as a single system. Skipping this step leads to piecemeal, out-of-context design that creates additional effort for the designer and confusion for the end user because both have to work extra hard to understand the full picture.

- **Route monitoring**: As shoppers move through the mall, they continue encountering maps identical to the one from earlier, except for one noticeable difference. The icon showing your location has changed, as noted by the arrow in the following image. This is route monitoring, which also includes and accounts for the previous two characteristics of orientation and route decision:

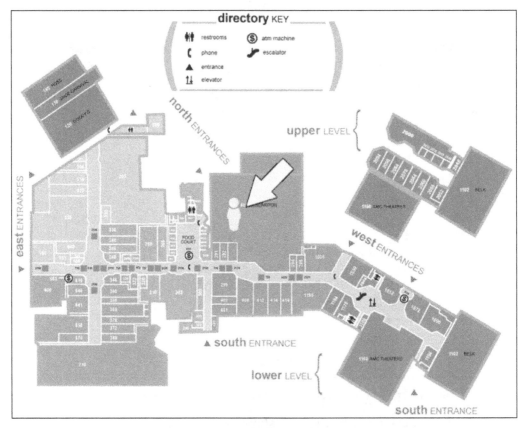

Source: http://m.mallseeker.com/m/i/map/tallahassee-mall-map.jpg

In an online setting, route monitoring might be breadcrumbs, a progress indicator or perhaps even a listing of what you looked at previously and new items inspired by your previous purchases. The following image demonstrates some of these design types visually.

These subtle reminders provide users with a sense that the system knows where they are and can help them if they go off course or need to return later without having to start at the beginning. Providing guidance throughout an experience is comforting and gives users the confidence to explore, knowing that getting back on track will be easy.

- **Destination recognition**: When we finally arrive at our destination, we want to know. Ambiguity is not comforting. We want confirmation, as the following examples demonstrate:

Seamless IA

As technology improves and becomes more complex, good IA becomes more complex as well. Not only do we need to provide a great experience, we also need to be aware that these experiences don't always end when the user leaves the store or when they turn off their computers. In a constantly connected world, information is always moving and transcending from one medium to the next. As a result, IA and design is no longer about a single, isolated experience or a single journey. It is about moving seamlessly from one experience to the next. To explain this more clearly, let's look at one of the best examples of seamless IA.

It's no secret that Apple leads the way in innovation, usability, and IA — not to mention the excitement their products generate with customers. Apple's success is not an accident. For years, they have been listening to their customers and it shows. For example, consider Apple's website. It's sleek and super simple to navigate. It's also very much in keeping with their product line, which is minimalist, hip, and very easy to use and understand.

Apple's home page always promotes the newest items first, with other items presented lower down the page and at a different level of scale. All the images Apple uses to showcase their products are large, colorful, and ready for purchase. At the bottom of the page, you'll find another type of sitemap. This one is viewable by the user, providing a listing of other departments or sections of the site that are equally useful, but smaller in size to avoid distracting them from the more important information at the top.

Source: Apple.com

Apple's website succeeds because not only does it look great and is easy to use, but it also provides ample opportunity to explore and to discover new items in great detail without ever getting confused or lost.

Please refer back to the 10 Principles of Good Design from the previous chapter to see how Apple's website and mobile app designs hold up.

When you enter an Apple store, the user experience is very similar. Items are easy to find and presented in full color, ready to use and purchase with a swipe of a credit card. Simplicity is often synonymous with Apple products, and therefore, Apple has a high level of customer/user expectation to live up to, and they take this responsibility seriously.

For example, this image is the floor plan of every Apple store:

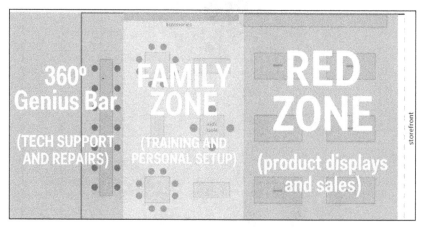

Source: http://www.businessinsider.com/apple-store-layout-makes-you-spend-2014-9

As you can see, it is divided into three sections:

- **Red Zone**: The entrance to the store is called the red zone. It's an open floor plan designed for wandering and exploring all of the cool devices Apple has to offer. There's even special lighting to make the products look more appealing. Should you want to make a purchase, just flag down an employee and they will swipe your credit card on the spot. No waiting in line and no time to change your mind.

- **Family Zone**: The next section is the green zone, or family zone, and provides free training to anyone who purchased an item. It also provides kid-related items placed at kid level for better eye contact. Is Apple manipulating its customers with these clever psychological tricks or is this just good IA at work? I'll let you be the judge, although it is hard to discount the effect.

Incidentally, supermarkets do this too. Walk down the cereal aisle and check out the faces staring back at you from the boxes. Supermarkets place kid cereal at kid level, meaning at a height where kids are most likely to see them. A study found that the characters on the cereal boxes are indeed looking downward, at an angle designed to engage in eye contact with the little ones, thus sealing the deal. — `http://www.cbsnews.com/news/cereal-box-characters-are-staring-at-your-children-study-says/`

Source: `www.scpr.org`

For the record, the faces on the adult cereal boxes look straight ahead:

Source: `http://sites.psu.edu/believeinyourself; www.quakeroats.com; https://coxrare.files.wordpress.com/2014/04/adult-cereal.jpg; https://ethicsofdesign.files.wordpress.com/2013/03/new-quakerlogo_4cp_med_jan-2012.jpg`

Creepy? Perhaps. Effective? Absolutely! But, I digress.

The blue zone, also known as the 360 genius bar, rounds out Apple's seamless IA experience is the third and final section. Regardless of how you may feel about the level of genius in the genius bar, this section is designed to look like the concierge desk of a Ritz Carlton hotel—a hotel synonymous with high-end clientele and services and thereby creating—creating a psychological connection of high-end quality and service.

The Apple store also provides a lot of distractions. Take a moment to think about them or notice them the next time you are in the store. Also notice how enjoyable they are and how easy it is to make a purchase using Apple's EasyPay app and avoiding long lines. Of course, every store has its share of customer horror stories and bad experiences, but overall, Apple usually does not disappoint.

Four C's exercise

Think about the four Cs of IA and how they are present throughout the seamless Apple online/store experience. Try filling in the blanks

- Coordination:
- Cooperation:
- Change:
- Consequence:

Remember, there are no wrong answers, only effective solutions.

More examples of good IA

We'll close this chapter with some additional examples of IA and see how you can put to use what you've learned in this chapter. However, before we do, I want to leave you with a final thought as you begin incorporating good IA into your design work:

> *There are two kinds of people: how people and what people. There are those who think about how they are going to accomplish something, and there are those who stop to think about what it is they want to accomplish in the first place…What and how are important in doing almost anything. I try to think of what is to be done rather than how to do it. It's important to consciously state: "No, that's a how, not a what; think of what it is and not how you're going to do it."*
>
> *–Richard Saul Wurman, Hats, Design Quarterly 145*

Creating good IA and good UX design requires knowing *what* you want to convey and *what* you want your customers/users to accomplish. This should be done before you start to consider *how* you are going to do it. Compare your work to the techniques learned here—wayfinding, fractal loading, seamless IA, the four Cs, taxonomy—and test them with real users to experiment, learn, and improve your work before presenting it to a larger population. Most importantly, remember that just because *you* understand your design, that doesn't mean everyone else will. This cannot be stressed enough. Know well who you are designing for, guide them, inform them, help them, then sit back, watch how well they do, learn from them and improve.

Amazon

For 20 years, Amazon has led the way in designing a highly usable website experience that adheres to all the topics discussed in this chapter. It's hard to know where to begin when discussing Amazon's IA, so we'll start at the most logical place, their home page:

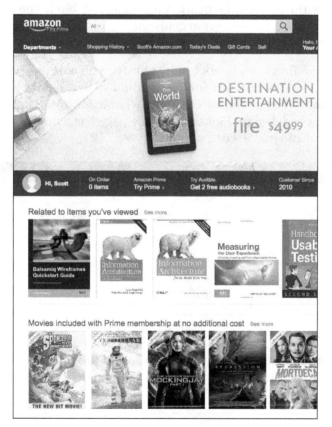

Source: Amazon.com

On any given day, Amazon's home page displays an array of products, much of which is presented especially for you and me. Amazon, like most well-designed sites, gives their customers/users the impression that they know us personally and display what we want to see, based on our previous interactions on the site. It is also impossible to get lost among their many distractions as you explore and learn. If you get disoriented, Amazon provides ample feedback, alerting you to your present location and guiding you easily back on track to your original objective. As for the four Cs, can you see how Amazon **coordinates** information and how **cooperative** its IA is with our every move? Do you notice how often **change** occurs on Amazon's site and how often they add new features? Has this ever interfered with your ability to complete a task? As for consequences, does Amazon succeed in providing an experience that delivers? They are not dominating the online and offline marketplace for nothing.

LinkedIn

Like Twitter, LinkedIn is a useful tool and very engaging, but if you don't understand how to use it, it could seem confusing. Like Twitter, LinkedIn is also filled with profiles that never gain traction, while others drive careers forward.

In terms of IA, LinkedIn's framework is very sturdy, with a design to match. When you look around LinkedIn, whether for the first time or as a regular user, there is a lot going on. It may even be difficult to know what to look at first. However, this does not mean it's a bad design. LinkedIn's home page has a number of different choices that the user can make. For example:

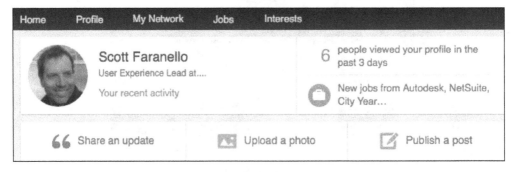

Source: LinkedIn.com

Choosing a path on LinkedIn's home page is easy and provides very intuitive and clear destination recognition. This is how LinkedIn works in terms of the four Cs.

Coordination

LinkedIn coordinates information quite well. Its site mapping allows a user to create a profile, connect and communicate with others, write articles, share job history, follow and like articles and posts, review colleagues, find a job, join groups with similar interests, and have fun doing it! For example, the more information you provide, the higher is your ranking:

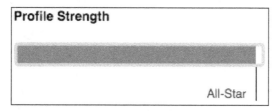

Source: `LinkedIn.com`

You can also track who has viewed your profile and see how you rank against others in your network and your field:

Source: `LinkedIn.com`

The type of interaction seen here is referred to as **gamification**, in which designers look for ways to engage users with additional incentives.

In terms of taxonomy, LinkedIn provides great search capabilities, which you can filter as you type. LinkedIn uses the **Search for people, jobs, companies, and more** heading. Combinations will also work with varying degrees of success. If you want to get really into the weeds, their advanced search is there when you need it and can filter down to the narrowest criteria.

Cooperation

Like Twitter and many other websites that are social in nature, cooperation is imperative. To do this well requires incentive—the kind that speaks to customers/ users in a way that they can understand. A site like LinkedIn provides a very specific offering, and in order for it to take off and prosper, their UX designers need to understand fully who their users are and what they want and need from a site like this. Considering that LinkedIn has become synonymous with professional networking, it's a testament to their success. At present, there are 414 million registered users—that's two new users per second! They are also in 200 countries and territories.—`http://expandedramblings.com/index.php/by-the-numbers-a-few-important-linkedin-stats/`.

LinkedIn's interface and behind-the-scenes architecture is also highly cooperative. Updating a profile, posting an article, connecting with others and joining a group are all easy to do and instantaneous to create. The only time required is based on how much information you what to share.

Change

LinkedIn is essentially a social-networking tool. As a result, it changes minute by minute. You will always find something new on LinkedIn and when something new appears there is no relearning required, or learning that requires much time to understand. The site also adds functionality and features that, unlike Facebook, you don't hear people complain about. Change should always be an improvement, not a refactoring. Usability is about ease of learning and ease of accomplishing tasks. That is what makes for good UX and good IA.

Consequence

The user statistics I shared earlier from LinkedIn are a testament to its usefulness. In fact, this book is the consequence of the connections I made using LinkedIn. If you are not yet a part of the community, take the time to join and start making connections. If you need help getting the most out of this very effective tool, let me know!

Another consequence of LinkedIn and other successful websites is that they all have something to teach us. Regardless of how often you visit these websites, it is important to understand why many other people do and then leverage that information as you forge your own path to better design. Remember, just because you don't like something doesn't mean it's bad. Everything can teach us something, as the following quote demonstrates:

"We used to drive around Michigan on Woodward Avenue. I remember one time a Cowsill's song came on the radio and I said 'turn that crap off'. Bob said, 'No, wait Glenn, they are on the radio and we are not. Let's listen to how they got there. –
`http://womc.cbslocal.com/2013/03/05/glenn-frey-talks-bob-seger-and-woodward-avenue/"`

Internet movie database

Internet movie database (IMDb) is one of my favorite time wasters. After watching a movie, I usually go directly to IMDb to read the Trivia section as well as the goofs—the mistakes the movie's editors failed to notice. IMDb is full of information, and it appears to include a listing for every movie ever made, along with ratings and reviews—even for the bad ones!

Source: `http://www.imdb.com/title/tt4009460/`

If you were wondering, tAs of this writing, this is considered to be the lowest rated movie of all times in IMDb's database. Consider yourself warned!

IMDb is loaded with distractions, and that's a good thing! It also provides great search functionality, allowing users to find any movie in seconds, by title, by actor name, and by a number of other criteria as part of their search taxonomy:

Source: `http://www.imdb.com`

In addition, there are a number of other categories with one-click access:

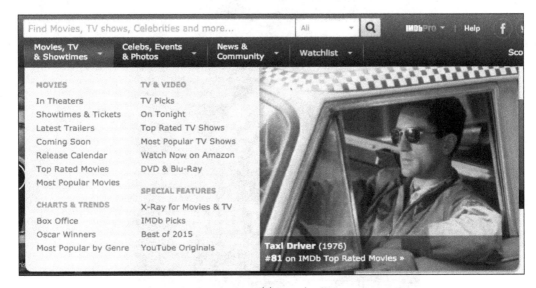

Source: `http://www.imdb.com`

IMDb is also a great example of the four Cs, with well-coordinated information that is highly cooperative, not only with regards to how the information interacts and interconnects, but also in terms of user engagement. Their **News & Community** section makes participation fun and provides movie aficionados a place to show their movie knowledge. Even at a quick glance, IMDb also demonstrates design made for change. With about 600 movies made each year in Hollywood, not including independent films and documentaries, IMDb has to make room for all of them. Lastly, the consequence of IMDb's IA is an ever growing movie encyclopedia and the go-to destination for all things film!

 Check out for yourself how IMDb is a great example of good IA and good UX design. Visit: www.imdb.com/

Closing thoughts

The Internet is filled with good IA and bad. Knowing how to identify which is which and transferring that knowledge to your own design and IA work is what will separate good IA from bad. IA is not something to dabble in or to put off until a later time. It requires serious attention and thought. Before considering a design solution, identify *what* you want to convey before you consider *how* you are going to do it. Piles of data and content are useless unless your users can understand and interact with it, and design is useless unless it has a strong IA driven by a well thought out sitemap and a holistic understanding of the larger whole of the design.

If you find yourself designing the look and feel before IA, then it is time to change course. Begin with IA, create a sitemap, and make sure to think about each of the IA strategies presented in this chapter and then test them with real users. Designing good IA can be a challenge, but before long, you will begin to see improvements, not only in your design work, but also in the way your customers/users respond to a great experience.

Summary

In this chapter, we focused on the foundations of IA to better understand how good IA guides customers/users to a desired outcome. We introduced **The Four Cs of IA**—a checklist of sorts to help validate your IA work and how to identify them across a wide variety of designs, both online and off. We also learned from example the presence of IA in our everyday lives and how that translates online. We looked at mental models and taxonomy and how understanding how your customers/users think is vital for guiding them to their desired decision. We looked at sitemaps and how important they are for understanding the complete design experience from a high level. We looked at how IA exists all around us, from cities to supermarkets to wherever a person needs to interact and understand information quickly and easily. We looked at IA as maps and how Wayfinding helps to guide users to their destination with care. Finally, we looked at seamless IA and how this connectivity allows IA to coexist in different environments and provide consistent transition and the continuous flow of information.

Coupled with a mindset for UX to solve the problems of your end users, IA, like good design, is a natural step in your process to improve your design work. It is also one that cannot be put off until a later time and certainly not ignored. You are now another step closer and another strategy stronger towards becoming a better and more mature UX practitioner and designer. We will continue on the path in the next chapter as we look at UX maturity, what it means and how to get there.

5

Patterns, Properties, and Principles of Good UX Design

"Patterns can exist in the world, only to the extent that it is supported by other patterns...When you build a thing you cannot merely build that thing in isolation, but must also repair the world around it, and within it, so that the larger world at that one place becomes more coherent, and more whole; and the thing which you make takes its place in the web of nature, as you make it."

This quote, written by architect and educator Christopher Alexander, comes from his highly influential book, entitled *A Pattern Language: Towns, Buildings, Construction*. In the book, Alexander posited that good design communicates to us on a subconscious level using a language of its own. This is not a spoken language. It is the language of patterns, which are communicated through the connection we feel when we are in their presence.

"There is a central quality which is the root criterion of life and spirit in a man, a town, a building, or a wilderness. This quality is objective and precise, but it cannot be named."

– Christopher Alexander

The objective quality that *cannot be named* is central to the concept of good design, because good design is absolutely verifiable on some level, even when we can't explain it. Alexander believed that we inherently recognize good design, because we have been exposed to it in nature. Since we have been exposed to nature our whole lives, we therefore recognize and respond to similar patterns in man made design. Alexander called this experience *wholeness*. It is best described as that which makes us feel alive, present, and connected to whatever we are interacting with.

UX designers use patterns to define solutions, solve problems, and create templates to deliver consistency, but this is only half the picture. The other half is becoming aware of natural patterns innate to the unconscious brain and incorporating them consciously into your design work. To demonstrate this, Alexander created the *Fifteen Fundamental Properties of Wholeness*, which we will look at now.

In this chapter we will look at:

- The fifteen fundamental properties of wholeness, as they apply to UX design
- How these properties will improve your UX design work
- How to create "wholeness" and "centeredness" in your UX design work using patterns

Patterns in UX design

Like we saw in the previous chapter and throughout this book, good design is everywhere, ever present, and takes on many forms. Often, the best design goes unnoticed, because it satisfies our needs and delivers on our expectations. It is only when design fails that it becomes noticeable. For example, when a submitted online form acknowledges a successful submission we move on, because we expected that:

Source: `https://support.formstack.com/customer/portal/articles/1930012-submit-actions`

It is only design does not acknowledge us for our efforts that we begin to notice.

As UX practitioners, our job is to drive customers/users to where they want to go, using design as a way to control it. When we are successful, we are essentially behavior modifiers, creating an environment as well as a system that is easy to navigate, understand, and follow. When we accomplish this, we have created something of value, a system that can stand on its own.

Christopher Alexander explained it this way:

> *"The system as a whole — that is to say, its pattern — is the thing, which we generally think of when we speak about something as a whole. Although the system of centers is fluid, and changes from time to time as the configuration and arrangement and conditions all change. Still, at any given moment, these centers form a definite pattern. This pattern of all the centers appearing in a given part of space — constitutes the wholeness of that part of space. It is this structure, which is responsible for its degree of life."*
>
> *– Christopher Alexander, The Search for Beauty,* `dreamsongs.com/Files/AlexanderPresentation.pdf`

If you recall "PICNIC" or *problem in chair, not in computer*, from *Chapter 1, The User Experience Mindset,* to blame bad design on the user is to ignore the errors we, as designers, committed, by failing to pattern our work on design patterns that already exist. Our job, therefore, if we want to improve as designers, is to learn how to see the patterns more clearly.

The 15 fundamental properties of wholeness

To understand Alexander's properties as the author intended them, there are many resources available. There are also a number of interpretations. What follows are interpretations of the 15 properties from a UX perspective, along with quotes from Alexander's work that will help you gain some context as to the author's original meaning. What you will find is that as you learn about and understand each property, you will come away with a more profound perspective of design and how incorporating these properties the patterns more into your work can deliver a more natural, balanced, centered, and ultimately, a more whole experience for you as a designer and for your customers/users as the recipients of your work.

Similar to Dieter Ram's *Ten Principles of Good Design* from *Chapter 3, Good UX Design,* the goal of these properties is to learn them, understand them, identify them, and start using them in your design work. How you use them and in what order is up to you.

Christopher Alexander's *The Fifteen Fundamental Properties of Wholeness*:

- Levels of Scale
- Strong Centers
- Boundaries
- Alternating Repetition
- Positive Space
- Good Shape
- Local Symmetries
- Deep Interlock
- Contrast
- Graded Variation
- Roughness
- Echoes
- The Void
- Inner Calm
- Not-Separateness

 To see the 15 properties in their original form as Alexander defined them, read his books or visit http://www.tkwa.com/fifteen-properties/ for a wonderful interpretation.

Levels of Scale

Levels of scale allow for multiple centers to exist at once, and in such a way that they give the illusion of balance in order to present a single, larger whole. For example, here is a level of scale in action in the form of Incan stonework, Palace of Inca Roca, Cuzco, Peru:

Source: `http://www.ancient-code.com/wp-content/uploads/2015/09/`
`CUSCO-3-0024.jpg`

These massive hand-cut stones have been standing for centuries—a testament to the builder's skills, no doubt. It is important to note that these stones were placed by hand and without the use of mortar. These ancient builders understood that placing various sized stones atop one another would create a highly supportive structure that would withstand the test of time and remain a thing beauty for future generations to marvel at.

While our work as UX designers cannot compete with the Incas, we can still learn from them. Using our UX skills, we can build structure and strength in our design work as well, using design techniques such as various font sizes, headlines, subheaders, imagery, text, colors, IA, page flows, and smooth transitions. However, just piling it on is not what we are going for. We are going for a balanced system of *centers*, a *wholeness* that can support all the multiple elements—weight, size, shape, flow. They together create meaning and understanding about how the rest of the environment functions.

In the world of UX design, we see levels of scale playing out all the time. For example, we can see it in this seemingly benign design:

Source: http://s.numrush.nl/wp-content/uploads/2014/06/ios-8-weather-1.jpg

Here, we can see many levels of scale and many *centers* or areas for our eyes to focus on. As a whole, this design provides the user with all the information they need at a glance. It starts with today's weather and location, in both text and imagery. Then, the design moves downward in direction and scale, until we reach the bottom, where we see information about the stakeholders of the app — Yahoo, The Weather Channel — the ones, you could say, supporting this application.

Levels of scale:

- Directs eye movement
- Provides hierarchy and priority
- Directs our attention and focus

- Tells us what to do first
- Acts as a map
- Provides the shape, strength, balance and integrity of the entire design.
- Levels our expectations

Levelling our expectations

With regards to this last one, we can see it played out with responsive design, as elements of scale degrade and shift as they move from one device and screen size to another. Responsive design could be the equivalent of a crumbling wall if not planned, prepared, and cared for with utmost respect. Remember too that responsive design is only responsive when it actually responds to its environment and has a design foundation strong enough to support it.

Source: https://www.oho.com/sites/default/files/MVG-responsive.png

To provide for this foundation requires understanding the mediums in which your work will appear, planning what those designs will look like, and preparing the foundation so your design will accommodate each one separately as well as a coherent system. Remember, in many cases you are dealing with more than just design. There are also backend, proprietary, and internal systems that have their own coding requirements and restrictions. Work within those restrictions before you begin designing and test your work to make sure its visual *center* will hold up. This brings us to the next property.

Strong centers

> *"Like levels of scale, the concept of a strong center is recursive; it does not refer to [some] grand center, but to the fact that at a great variety of scales, in a thing which is alive, we can feel the presence of a center, and that it is this multiplicity of different centers, at different levels, which engages us."*

> *Alexander, Christopher. The Nature of Order: An Essay on the Art of Building and the Nature of The Universe, Book One, The Phenomenon of Life. Berkeley, Calif.: Center for Environmental Structure, 2002.*

Throughout this book, the word **foundation** has appeared numerous times to make the point that good design begins and ends with a strong focal point or central starting place from which you can begin designing. It is this focal point that becomes the "center" of your design, the place from which everything else is built upon and where the customer/user and designer can always return. For example, here is an aerial photo of Central Park, New York City:

Source: http://www.dailyoverview.com/leisuregallery/

This incredible marvel of engineering was designed to provide city dwellers with a reprieve from the noise, crowds, and stress of the big city. Once in the park, the city literally disappears, allowing park dwellers to enjoy the serene landscape and other attractions. Designed by American landscape architect Frederick Law Olmsted, the park became the model for urban parks and notably holds the title for the most visited urban park in the United States. — https://en.wikipedia.org/wiki/Central_Park.

The attraction we have to the *center* is not just found in city park design. It is everywhere and at every level of scale—from town centers to building architecture to the layout of the rooms within them, right down to the furniture. Design with strong centers naturally draw us in, create a sense of community, and invites playful activity. In UX design, we see strong centers as website landing pages, such as Google, or your iPhone or Android's home screen. From there, almost anything is possible.

Source: `https://www.apple.com/support/assets/images/products/iphone/` `hero_iphone_6s_2x.png`

But, the center does not stop at the main "home" level. For example:

- At the highest level, the phone itself is the center. We can barely put it down, and we return to it nearly every waking minute of the day and night. Our phones literally guide and, in a way, control our day.

- The next center is the home screen, centering on the day, date, time, battery life, and connectivity. In other words, it contains the essentials on which the rest of our activities with our devices relies upon.

- A level down from there is the app center, arranged to our preference for quick, efficient, effective and satisfying usage.

- From there, each app contains its own center and so on.

- As we saw in the previous property, *Levels of Scale*, centers do not stop at any one particular level. However, they are only effective when all the surrounding centers point back to the larger whole, creating order and organization, direction, and a pull back to it. Centers create a sense of balance and boundary that allow the entire design to hold together.

Boundaries

"Wherever two very different phenomena interact, there is also a "zone of interaction" which is a thing in itself, as important as the things which it separates."

Alexander, Christopher. The Nature of Order:

Boundaries create space and join elements together, while keeping them separate at the same time. Boundaries also help clarify and create form — the stronger the boundary, the stronger the form. Here is a familiar example of boundaries:

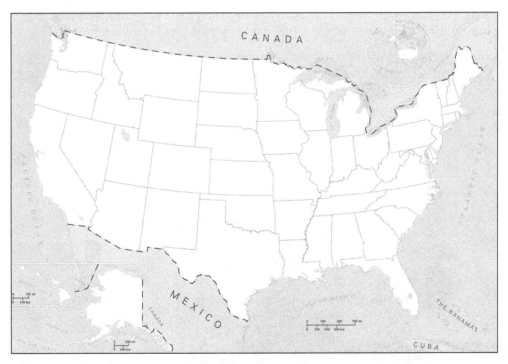

Source: https://upload.wikimedia.org/wikipedia/commons/8/8c/US_state_outline_map.png

Notice how each boundary scales as well, with each becoming its own "center" of wholeness the closer you get. For example:

- Globe
- Continent
- Country
- Region
- State
- City
- Town/village
- District
- Street
- Address

And so on.

UX design requires boundaries too. Boundaries in design creates order, organization, and help viewers focus on an area, both at a high level and closer to "the ground". For example, here are a few designs that make good use of boundaries:

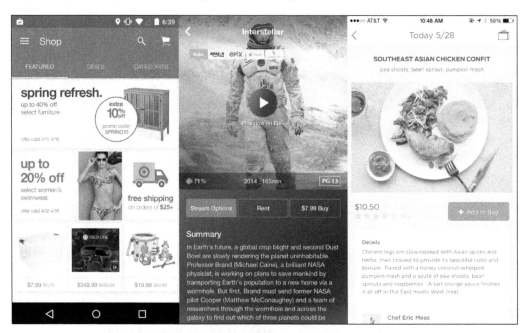

Source: http://cdn.pttrns.com/341/4667_f.jpg;
http://cdn.pttrns.com/341/5889_f.jpg;
http://images.mobile-patterns.com/1433281975865-2015-05-28%2010.48.47.png

Notice the separation in each design between sections and how your eye is drawn to different areas of focus. Also notice the centers within each. The first image has a center that pulls you directly to the items for purchase, while the second image prefers the you interact with the **play** button and the **Rent** button below it. While I am sure purchasing this movie is desired by the designer and the stakeholder, but, based on the design, my guess is that renting a movie is the more preferable choice. All three images also make use of boundaries in terms of visual demarcation between areas, using shading, colors, scale, font size, weight, and so on. Also, notice how these effects create centers of their own. This is, of course, not new or unique to design, but it is a sign of good design. In fact, if you go back to review any of the examples of good design used throughout this book, you will find all of these properties and patterns at work.

Testing boundaries

Here is a very familiar design element, known as the hamburger menu:

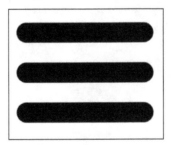

Like it or hate it, the hamburger menu has become one of the most highly used patterns in the digital realm, creating a lot of debate as well, with regard to its usefulness and intuitiveness. One of the debates has been around whether the understandability of this pattern could be improved. In a study using three variations of the hamburger menu, the bordered image was clicked significantly more often than either of the images without borders:

Source: http://exisweb.net/wp-content/uploads/2014/02/hamburgertest1.gif

It was further concluded that by adding a boundary, the image looked more like a button, a concept familiar to most users, thus drawing the eye to it.

To read more about this test and to see additional tests on this design, visit http://exisweb.net/mobile-menu-abtest.

Safe boundaries

If you recall from *Chapter 3, Good UX Design*, we talked about *safety* as an important element of good design. We can see it in pattern properties as well. In late 2014, Apple changed the wording on certain apps from **Free** to **GET**:

Source: http://cdn.macrumors.com/article-new/2014/11/getpurchasebutton. jpg

This was done to alert people downloading these apps that the app itself is free, users will encounter something called in-app purchasing offers. These are icons, banners, and buttons that suddenly appear on screen as you are in the middle of play. In reality, these are advertisements and in some cases, clicking on them can turn into an unwanted charge on your bill.

To clarify the issue even further, Apple added a line of text below the app name that said, **Offers in-App Purchases** to avoid unnecessary and annoying surprises later:

Source: `http://cdn.macrumors.com/article-new/2014/11/getpurchasebutton.jpg`

This type of boundary is important because it creates a layer of protection and additional security for the user, almost like a moat around a medieval castle, always on the lookout for threats to the user's experience.

Alternating Repetition

> *"Repetition which occurs in things which have life is a very special kind of repetition. It is a kind where the rhythm of the centers that repeat is underlined, and intensified, by an alternating rhythm interlocked with the first and where a second system of centers also repeats, in parallel. The second system of centers then intensifies the first system, by providing a kind of counterpoint, or opposing beat."*

When we think about repetition, we often think of patterns repeating over and over again. While this is true, it is also true that for every visible pattern in positive space, there is a secondary pattern in negative space.

The following painting by M.C. Escher demonstrates this quite nicely:

Source: http://flyeschool.com/sites/flyeschool/files/images/art_terms/
escher6.jpg

At first glance, the lighter colors stand out more prominently than the darker ones, creating visible patterns with seemingly negative space in between. However, upon closer inspection, the dark matter has form of its own, creating an entirely new pattern and a very engaging design as a result. Here are some other repetitive pattern types to think about as you design. They are: regular, random, progressive, and flowing.

Regular repetition

Predictable. Consistent. Colors and visual elements may change, but the overall design maintains a steady pattern. There is uniformity and order as well. Everything is aligned and focuses the eye where the design wants it to go. Any change to a regular, repetitive pattern is used to create greater emphasis and focus, as shown in the following screenshot:

Source: http://www.mobile-patterns.com

In the examples in the preceding image, this type of repetition can be seen in the highlighting of the day of the week for quick viewing, the **Sign Up** and **Sign In** buttons and the regular/repetitive nature of the vertical display of the days of the week.

Random repetition

Random repetition lacks consistency in the rhythm or flow of a pattern, however, keep in mind, if you design with random repetition although a pattern may look random, but there should always be a valid design reason behind it:

Source: bobbyowsinski.blogspot.com;blog.spoongraphics.co.uk;
http://tieic.com/patterns-for-cobble-sett-laying/

While the various examples in the previous images may look random, each is by design, in nature, by a composer or an architectural designer. Seen separately, each element has no real meaning. Seen as a whole, each can be intrinsically beautiful to behold.

Progressive repetition

Progressive repetition is design presented as a progression of steps. This could be a staircase, a sign-up process on a website, or the steps taken to purchase an item online. The ultimate goal of this pattern type is to guide the user steadily towards their goal:

Starbucks Mobile App Screenshots from my iPhone

It may be difficult to see in the preceding images, but each screen takes the user progressively closer to their order in smooth, seamless and a natural flow, which is the next type of repetition.

Flowing repetition

Flowing repetition means natural movement, or natural flow, as this picture of sand dunes demonstrates:

Source: `http://wallperswide.com/desert_sand_dunes-wallpapers.html`

The key thing to remember about flowing repetition is to make sure your design provides a sense of forward movement. Here are some examples:

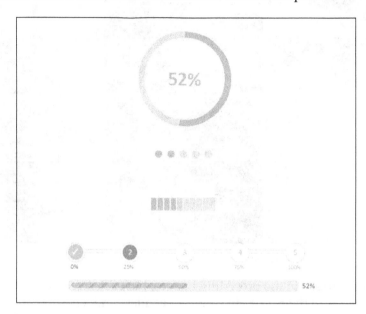

Source: http://www.formget.com/wp-content/uploads/2015/01/progress-bar-type-.png

Similar to the preceding property, *progressive repetition,* designers often use graphical displays to alert users of their progress in completing tasks. The examples in the preceding image demonstrate this. By helping the customer/user to see that they are moving forward successfully you are ensuring that they stay engaged and connected to the message you are trying to convey.

Positive space

> "*The definition of positive space is straightforward: every single part of space has positive shape as a center. There are no amorphous meaningless leftovers.*"

When design has purpose, there is no meaningless space. Any space that exists is positive space, acting like an invisible bridge, connecting one element to the next and drawing the user in to the experience. In design, positive space is often referred to as *whitespace*. Comedians call positive space *timing*, that pause before the punch line, placed so carefully that a second longer or shorter and the joke falls flat. Musicians call positive space "rests". They are used to create a similar mood, and timing is equally essential. Of course, you would know from experience if you have ever tried comedy, music, or any art form that it is not easy and requires much practice before it could be fully understood and internalized.

However, like all the concepts presented throughout this book, once you begin to see more clearly what is actually occurring as a result, your design will take on more meaning, not only as a designer, but for your customers/users too. As an example of positive space, here is an image you may have seen:

Source: `http://webdesign.tutsplus.com/articles/using-white-space-or-negative-space-in-your-designs--webdesign-3401`

Do you see a finely shaped vase or two faces? Or both? What about the next image:

Source: `https://shannanovak.wordpress.com/2013/02/04/use-of-positive-and-negative-space/`

In order for both of the preceding images to work and to create mood and meaning, there is no leftover space. The black and white shapes are interconnected and virtually inseparable. Here's another one:

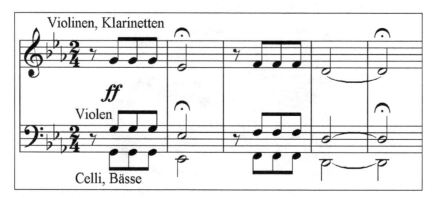

Source: https://masterworksfestival.org/wp-content/uploads/2016/02/Blog-4a.png

Even if you don't know how to read music, you would know this rhythm when you heard it. It's the opening to Beethoven's fifth Symphony, better known as "da-da-da-DAH, da-da-da-DAH". Each note, each rest, the time signature, and so on are all working together to create positive space and, as a result, beautiful, listenable, and very approachable, engaging music.

Good UX design relies on the same approach. What we do not place on the page is just as important as what we place there. It is within this space that information becomes organized and quite literally provides meaning to the viewer, consciously or otherwise. Here is an example:

Source: http://www.google.com

Here is another example:

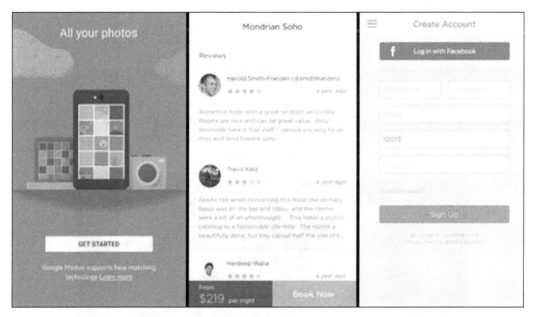

Source: http://www.mobile-patterns.com/

In each of the images in the preceding example, there is no wasted space.
Everything on the page has meaning and purpose, guiding the user to a
destination and a clear outcome.

Alexander refers to positive space as:

> "*swelling until it meets the others, each one having its own positive shape caused
> by its growth as a cell from the inside.*"

–https://www.dreamsongs.com/Files/AlexanderPresentation.pdf

I interpret this in terms of online social engagement design as it swells to meet the
others, that is, the people using the design to connect and engage on a large scale.
I also interpret "positive" space it as something inherent to all good design, where
customers/users can interact and engage easily, effectively, efficiently and to
their satisfaction.

Good Shape

> *"A good shape is a center which is made up of powerful intense centers, which have good shape themselves."*

Everything has shape, and we are bombarded with shapes every moment of our lives. While we don't often acknowledge shapes, unless they are strikingly different from what we are used to seeing, but at a subconscious level, we are referencing shapes all the time. It is literally how we make sense of the world around us. Shapes are everywhere. From a favorite chair to the way the sun enters a room, shape has a power of its own to convey a message and meaning.

Source: https://beardedhac.wordpress.com/tag/light-through-a-window/

In the field of UX design, we often refer to shape and our recognition of it as affordances — the relationship between an object to its environment and our ability to understand the action to take as a result. For example, if you saw these two objects together, you would probably know what to do:

Source: `http://worldwanders.com/tcomp/B%20plug.jpg`

The preceding image is also another great example of positive and negative space working together.

 This is a good time to mention that although each of these properties are discussed separately, as you come to understand them, look for them within each other as well.

Here is an example of good shape in UX design:

Source: `http://www.mobile-patterns.com`; `http://www.mobilemozaic.com`

Notice how the images in the preceding examples convey meaning instantly while also drawing your attention to other properties as well, like levels of scale, positive and negative space, repetition, and so on. What others can you see?

To a large degree, patterns are essentially the accumulation of good shapes that are familiar to us. By putting these shapes together, we create patterns and pattern libraries that allow us to reuse good shapes repeatedly. Good shapes also give us the confidence to make at least a strong assumption regarding how recognizable and usable these shapes will be and their meaning. Of course, you still need to test your assumptions with actual users, but then you already knew that, didn't you?

Local Symmetries

"Perfect symmetry is often a mark of death in things, rather than life"

Symmetry is perhaps best described as any shape that can be divided, reflected, rotated, and scaled without losing its original shape, even if only one half of the shape is visible. In psychology, this is known as "gestalt" in which "the mind forms a global whole" even if only one half is visible. — https://en.wikipedia.org/wiki/ Gestalt_psychology. Symmetry can occur across an entire design or within smaller areas of a design where symmetry becomes localized, regardless of the larger whole. Alexander demonstrated this using the example of Spain's *Palace of Alhambra*:

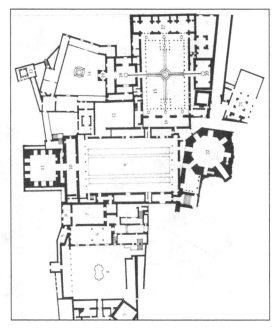

Source: http://www.livingneighborhoods.org/pics/fifteen/alhambraplan.jpg

Alexander described Alhambra this way:

> *"The plan of Alhambra…is a marvel of centers formed in a thousand combinations, and yet with beautiful symmetrical order at every point in space."*

Here is another example of local symmetry:

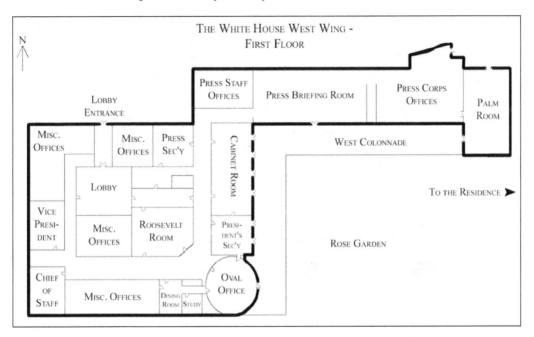

Source: https://commons.wikimedia.org/wiki/File:White_House_West_Wing_-_1st_Floor.png

We can utilize symmetry in UX design as well, in order to focus attention, create balance, and to convey importance in specific areas. There are few ways to represent this in your design work. Here are the various types of symmetry:

- **Reflective symmetry**: A mirrored image where both halves appear to be identical.

- **Rotational or radial symmetry**: Elements that rotate about a center point, that is, bicycle tire spokes, petals on a flower, and so on.

- **Translational symmetry**: Repeating elements or a repeating sequence that moves in a specific direction.

Refer to the following images for examples of each:

Source: `http://images.northrup.org/picture/xl/swan/swan-reflection-vertical.jpg`; `publicdomainpictures.net`; `pixabay.com/en/sit-grandstand-theater-139661/`

In UX design, symmetry can be represented using all three categories as well, albeit with some variation, as shown in the following examples:

Source: `http://www.mobile-patterns.com`; `http://www.mobilemozaic.com`

In the first image in the preceding example, we can see a UX design version of reflective symmetry as each row of thumbnail images reflects the row below, and so on. While the images change, the basic form and function stays constant. The image in the center demonstrates rotational or radial symmetry more clearly, where the information in the center becomes the center point, while the surrounding "petals" become the visual indicator of interaction and forward movement. Finally, in the third image, we see translational symmetry in the form of side bar navigation, repeating each element as it moves down the page. Of course, these are just a few examples. Don't stop here! Find some more. They become more visible once you start to look for them.

Deep Interlock and Ambiguity

> *"Living structures contain some form of interlock: situations where centers are "hooked" into their surroundings. The center and its surroundings interpenetrate each other, using intermediate centers, which belong to both of the two adjacent larger centers."*

As the name implies, deep interlock creates an ambiguous area between two centers, forming a third center between them. In doing so, a sense of connectedness is created, where separate elements become one. The result is a more inviting, less threatening, and friendlier experience for the user. One of the best examples to demonstrate this can be found in the following image:

Source: https://pixabay.com/en/porch-rocking-chair-wood-relax-1034405/

This may look like just a wraparound porch, but is the porch inside or outside? It is actually a bit of both, providing protection from the elements while allowing the user to transition to the outdoor environment less abruptly. Deep interlock and ambiguity is literally a seamless transition from one environment to the next.

Here is an example closer to our focus area:

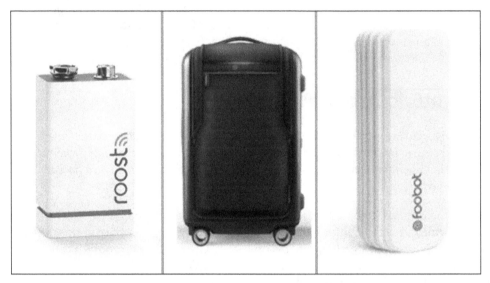

Source: http://iotlist.co/

From left to right, the items in preceding image are as follows:

- **Roost smart battery**: This delivers notifications to you wherever you are. In other words, this is not your average 9V battery.
- **Bluesmart connected carry-on**: With this, you can lock, weigh, and track your carry-on with your phone.
- **Foobot indoor air quality monitor**: This not only monitors the air quality of your home or office, it also sends alerts via the smartphone app if anything should change.

The examples in the preceding image demonstrate what we refer to as the Internet of Things or IoT, an approach to design that seamlessly interlocks multiple ideas and concepts to create a single, seamless experience for the user while at the same time transitioning our understating between what was familiar and what is new.

Contrast

"Life cannot occur without differentiation. Unity can only be created from distinctness."

How we approach contrast can lead to different outcomes. For example, while it is true that images, headlines, font size, and weight can pull focus and draw attention, that does not mean it is good design. On the other hand, when contrast works well, it can provide clarity, organization, and distinctness.

If you recall, in *Chapter 3*, *Good UX Design*, we looked at an example of native advertising and the challenges it posed in defining good design.

Source: http://www.wordstream.com/images/native-advertising-examples-vanity-fair-hennessy.jpg

Sure, the ad is attention grabbing and provides easy cues on how to interact with the information, but what value does it add to anyone other than advertisers hoping that the user clicks on it, be it on purpose or accidentally?

Alexander wrote, "Contrast has a unifying effect on the center." While this is true from a visual perspective, as UX designers, we have to remember that directing the user to where we want them to go is not always in their best interest. In other words, good UX design is also about balance, one that satisfies the business objective and the customer/user objective at the same time.

Let's look at the following example. Take a look at the contrast in these images:

Source: http://www.mobilemozaic.com; http://www.appreciateui.com

Let's review some of the factors that allow contrast to work effectively here:

- Balance and symmetry. No one element overtakes another.
- The eye is free to scan and choose based on interest and need rather than unnecessary or unpleasant distraction.
- Patterns are repeated to denote commonalities and consistency.
- Many of the other properties of wholeness are at work as well (See if you can find some of them in the preceding example).
- Imagery is used to quickly clarify and provide meaning.
- Visual separation makes page scanning easier and faster.
- Color palette complements, enhances, balances, and does not distract. If the user is thinking about the color more than the context, then it is a distraction.

[
 In addition to architecture and visual design, you can find the properties of wholeness in art and photography as well. For example, type into Google names such as `Mondrian`, `Matisse`, `Monet`, `Pollock`, `Gauguin` and photographers like `Ansel Adams`, `Henri Cartier Bresson`, and `Yousef Karsh`. Alternatively, simply type the term `photography contrast examples`. By learning from the greats and identifying how the properties of wholeness are at play, you will begin to see your design improve as a result.
]

"Learn the tunes by playing the masters, learn expression by playing yourself."

–DC DowDell

Gradients

"Unless the spaces in a building are arranged in a sequence which corresponds to their degrees of privateness, the visits made by strangers, friends, guests, clients, family, will always be a little awkward."

–Christopher Alexander, et al. A Pattern Language: Towns, Buildings, Construction.

Visual designers understand gradients to be the smooth blending of colors and shades to create the illusion of transition from one color/shade to the next. Educators use semantic gradients as a method of broadening and deepening students' understanding of related words. Architects use gradients to create varying degrees of intimacy, such as where to locate bedrooms, reading rooms, kitchen, den, and so on. Gradients add dimension and meaning to space and can influence encounters, meetings, and gatherings. — *Christopher Alexander, et al. A Pattern Language: Towns, Buildings, Construction.*

In UX design, gradients can influence movement, leading users through gradual, meaningful transitions, from one state to another. For example, in the following screenshot we can see three variations of gradient usage in the form of a progress wheel, slide to unlock and a brightness slider:

Source: `forum.xda-developers.com`; `https://www.smashingmagazine.com/2013/10/smart-transitions-in-user-experience-design/`;

Here are some additional gradient transition types that is often found in mobile design:

- **Fade**: This fades to the next page
- **Flip**: This flips to the next page from back to front
- **Flow**: This throws the current page away and comes in with the next page
- **Pop**: This goes to the next page like a pop-up window
- **Slide**: This slides to the next page from right to left
- **Slidefade**: This slides from right to left and fades in the next page
- **Slideup**: This slides to the next page from bottom to top
- **Slidedown**: This slides to the next page from top to bottom
- **Turn**: This turns to the next page

As with all of these properties, how you choose to use them is up to you. Just be sure to choose wisely.

Roughness

"It is certainly noticeable that all great buildings do have various small irregularities in them, even though they often conform to approximate overall symmetries and configurations. By contrast, buildings which are perfectly regular seem dead."

Roughness comes in all shapes and sizes. In architecture, roughness could be odd-shaped bricks making up a wall, raindrops on glass, or musical improvisation. Roughness is like drawing with a pen. Mistakes cannot be easily erased, nor do we want them to be. At the same time, what may appear random and haphazard is actually the result of deliberate imperfection, providing the listener/viewer/user with a more authentic, human experience. Roughness is conformity and adjustment to the situation at hand and doing so "without ego or contrived deliberation."— `http://www.tkwa.com/fifteen-properties/roughness-2/`.

In UX design, we find roughness too. For example, with responsive design, where "inhabitant and structure...mutually influence each other."— `http://alistapart.com/article/responsive-web-design`. We see it in app design as well where the designer wants to convey a sense of realism or an experience that feels unique and custom to the needs of the user. This is important because in the digital world it is easier to be precise than it is to be rough. Nevertheless, good UX design provides roughness when and where it is needed:

Source: `http://www.mobile-patterns.com`; `news.softpedia.com`;
`http://static-3.app4smart.me/uploads/posts/thumbs/1891/original-550da467e3.jpg`

In the preceding image we can see roughness played out in varying degrees. As various shapes, in the layout of a city in a GPS app, the placement of icons on a mobile screen to create a unique, custom landing page, and in game design, where roughness is created as a result of screen resolution or to convey an environment that immerses the user. Roughness is also the scattering of elements on the map, the ability to increase and decrease icon size on a mobile display, or the minimalist graphics of a mobile game to convey simplicity, ease simplicity and ease of use.

Echoes

> *"When echoes are present, the various smaller elements and centers, from which the larger centers are made, are all members of the same family; they contain echoes of one another; there are deep internal similarities between them which tie them together to form a single unity."*

In Alexander's world of architecture, an echo relates to repetition, where similar elements appear and reappear, but with small changes along the way. This property provides the user with a sense of familiarity throughout the design, delivering "a certain level of pleasure when encountering it." One of our goals as UX designers is to provide the customer/user with a sense of familiarity too, so that they can focus on their objective without any unpleasant disturbances. To reach this level of design quality requires a keen sense of the experience we want to create and the environment needed to achieve this. While we could reproduce Alexander's literal interpretation of echoes by repeating visual elements, UX design requires repetition in the form of patterns, in that they define an experience in terms of how it should function and *feel* to the end user. Through echoing, we also create design **consistency**.

When a customer/user engages with your design, there must be a feeling of familiarity almost immediately, as if they have done it before, even if they are using your design for the first time. By echoing familiar design elements in our work, we create a feeling of regularity, evenness, steadiness, stability, and trust—all traits we look for in leaders and what our customers/users look to us to provide as they are being led. Design patterns are all essentially echoes of what came before. They guide our design decisions without having to invent something new.

The Void

"There is a great lack of simple, silent, empty, large, calm space."

Recall, Times Square, NYC, from the previous chapter. Think about the noise, crowds, and distractions in that environment. The designs we create are spend their existence in a crowded city too, albeit a digital one, but nevertheless, an environment filled with a lot of noise and distraction too. Alexander referred to this noise as "the clutter of stuff." He also wrote about how to design around the clutter and in doing so create more "profound centers":

"In the most profound centers which have perfect wholeness, there is at the heart a void which is like water, infinite in depth, surrounded by and contrasted with the clutter of the stuff and fabric all around it."

The void is where the clutter and noise dissipates, allowing the design's "center" to cut through. The void is where we go to clear our heads, decompress, meditate, exercise, bang on drums and so on. The void is where clutter subsides and centeredness abounds. The void can also be a place, like a calm lake, a large empty courtyard, a park, or just a place of retreat where the clutter of the day simply falls away.

In UX design, the void is created when we provide an experience where goals and objectives are easily met, efficiently, effectively, and to the users satisfaction. The void is where the user goes to relax and enjoy the experience. The void is clutter free. The void, to put it simply, is good design.

Inner Calm

"The quality comes about when everything unnecessary is removed"

This is an easy one. Here, Alexander's talking about what we already know about good design: simplicity is what every designer strives for. It is also where inner calm emanates. Delivering anything else introduces clutter, user stress, and pulling away from the "center" where good design resides. Alexander explained inner calm as removing everything unnecessary and irrelevant. For UX designers, this could mean removing features, colors, images, links, content, and so on, until only the wireframe remains, and where only the most essential customer/user goals, tasks, and objectives remain. In design and development circles, this kind of scaled-down simplicity is referred to as a **Minimum Viable Product (MVP)**—a design consisting of only the most important interactions and elements. Design teams will often pursue an MVP approach when testing specific user scenarios and user interactions, in order to inform future development work.

Once an MVP is presented to users, any additional feature and functionality can be introduced later and incrementally so that we do not confuse, complicate, and clutter the design and the user's experience.

Not-Separateness

> *"When a thing lacks life, is not whole, we experience it as being separate from the world and from itself."*

The final property and perhaps the most significant is design that is inseparable from its surroundings. When design reaches this level, it does not draw attention to itself. It only provides for the user.

> *"I have discovered that the other fourteen ways in which centers come to life, will make a center which is compact, beautiful, determined, subtle – but, without this fifteenth property, are still often somehow strangely separate, cut off from what lies around it, lonely, awkward in its loneliness, too brittle, too sharp, perhaps too well delineated – above all too egocentric, because it shouts "Look at me, look at me, look how beautiful I am."*

> *–Christopher Alexander,* `https://www.dreamsongs.com/Files/ AlexanderPresentation.pdf`

Non-separateness design conjures up words like:

- Consistency
- Unity
- Peaceful
- Calm
- Complete
- Connected
- Centered
- Blended
- Smooth
- Belonging

In architecture, non-separateness is an open field blending into the horizon, a beach blending into the ocean, and so on. It is a building like The Empire State Building, an iconic building that literally defines New York City and is truly inseparable from its surroundings. Non-separateness is an automobile, inseparable from roads, street signs, traffic lights, and so on.

In UX design, non-separateness is our relationship to technology and our devices. It is the expectations of our customers/users that what we deliver and provide practical solutions to satisfy their needs. Non-separateness is also our relationship as designers and problem solvers to our customers/users, listening to them, hearing them, testing our assumptions with them and dispelling the myth of "faster horses" in the process.

Finding wholeness in your design work

Achieving the level of design that encompasses all 15 properties is no easy task, but it is worth your time to begin thinking about, noticing, and applying these properties to your design work immediately. Once you begin to notice them, you will find that they have been there all along. Incorporate some or all of them work and see if you notice a difference in how your customers/users respond.

As you do begin searching for these properties and incorporating them into your design work, ask yourself these questions:

- Does a building, website, or app make you feel more alive and more connected in some way? If so, why? Which properties are at play?

- How does incorporating these properties into your work affect your customer's/user's experience? Do you notice a change in their response to your designs after including some of these properties?

- Don't force these properties into your design work. Remember, always ask yourself, "how can I make this design feel more natural?"

- Is your design as simple as it can be? Is it the most basic design you can deliver, devoid of all unnecessary clutter? What can you take away without disrupting the user's experience and main objectives?

Challenge and inspire yourself, and as always, enjoy the journey.

Pattern libraries versus style guides

What's the difference between pattern libraries and styles guides and when should you use each? The answer depends on what stage of design you are in. For example, if you are wireframing (see *Chapter 7*, *Tools*, for more on wireframing), you will want to use patterns. Patterns are proactive design elements that help define and visualize interactions and information architecture.

Once you have completed the design phase, you are ready to create the **style guide**, a documentation of all your design decisions. The style guide will be used by the visual design and development teams to ensure that what they deliver is consistent with what you envisioned.

Both the pattern library and the style guide are living documents. As design changes occur, both should be updated accordingly.

 For additional resources on pattern libraries and style guides, see *Chapter 8, Final Thoughts and Additional Resources.*

Summary

In this chapter, you looked at the fifteen fundamental properties of wholeness, as they apply to UX design, how these properties will improve your design work and how to create "wholeness" and centeredness in your design work. Using multiple examples, we saw how patterns were created and how essential properties of design are incorporated into them. It is important to remember that these properties, while seemingly complex, are actually quite simple to recognize and use. Now that you know what to look for, finding them and incorporating them into your UX design work is now that much easier.

6

An Essential Strategy
for UX Maturity

*"Not having a measurement strategy is what keeps UX as a "nice to have"
as opposed to being an influential driving force within an organization."*

-http://uxrefresh.prosite.com/353189/www.markdisciullo.com

In the previous chapters, we focused on design fundamentals and how understanding and identifying them leads to better design decisions and ultimately better design solutions. We have also been looking at the importance of engaging our customers/users and dispelling the "faster horses" myth in the process. It should be obvious by now that close customer/user engagement is key to validating your design assumptions and producing better UX design, greater value and longer lasting solutions as a result.

While this is all extremely important, creating and delivering better UX solutions using foundational design techniques is only half of the story. The second half is about delivering results that your stakeholders, the ones who ultimately fund your projects, can clearly understand and benefit from. As you will see in this chapter, this requires an approach to UX on a level not often practiced, but one that is vital, not only for design longevity, but for career longevity as well.

In this chapter we will look at:

- The problem with UX maturity
- A different kind of UX approach
- Case studies proving the approach
- A UX maturity model that works

The problem with UX

If you have ever been in an interview for a UX role, you may have been asked the question, "What is your process?" It's an interesting question, but not a very useful one in most circumstances, because there is no right answer. No matter what you say or how detailed your process, it's only as good as the process of those with whom you are speaking. For example, if you are interviewing with a fast-paced agile team, you may get blank stares if you talk about lengthy research activities and usability studies. If you are interviewing with a slower-paced Waterfall UX team, you may not get a call back if you talk about minimally viable product design and adding features only when needed. In other words, every team has their own way of doing things, including UX. Expecting everyone to honor each other's processes is not something to readily depend on.

Another problem with UX maturity is not often discussed is that becoming a fully mature UX practitioner is less about designing *better* and more about working *smarter*. The common strategy among UX practitioners and teams today is to evangelize the importance of UX from a **qualitative** perspective, telling stakeholders how better UX design will improve customer/user satisfaction, usability and, as a result, user adoption, increased usage and ultimately, better business results.

Despite this approach, many companies do not fully understand the true value of UX in terms of what it really is and can really do for a company. As a result, UX is still looked at as the folks who do usability testing and create wireframes. In other words, while user satisfaction is important to stakeholders on some level, many UX teams, large and small are not able to provide the proof that UX actually provides a financially measurable, return on investment. Secondly, if UX is just wireframes and usability testing, many stakeholders think: *Why should we pay all that money for UX when the delivery team can do that? Besides, every time UX tells us how bad our work is it just creates more work for us. We don't have time or budget for such distractions".*

As a result, UX teams often wait for projects to come their way, fight for inclusion in customer facing projects, and do whatever it takes to keep up with the ever increasing efficiency and speed of agile development teams whose goal is to get products to customers/users at an ever increasing rate.

If any of this resonates, you are not alone. These problems have vexed UX practitioners and teams for years, causing stakeholders and entire companies to misunderstand its true value. If UX is to continue to evolve and continue to gain traction over the over the long term, then it is time to dispel another myth.

The UX process game

Open your web browser and use Google to look for the term "UPAposter". Then, click on the link that appears in the results. The link might look something like this:

> [PDF] UPA Usability Poster - mprove ✓
> www.mprove.de/script/00/**upa**/_media/**upaposter**_11x17.pdf ▾

Open the PDF document, and you will see a process map created by the **Usability Professional Association** (**UPA**), called *Designing the User Experience*, made to look like the *Chutes and Ladders* board game.

[Due to the risk of copyright infringement, I cannot display the image of the poster here. However, you could open the document in your browser as you continue reading.]

The UPA illustration does a fine job detailing the finer points of a typical UX process. However, once you try putting it into practice in a real-world project setting, you may find that many of the steps listed above need to be excluded or modified to fit with the schedule, budget, priorities, and goals of everyone else on the project and delivery team.

To test this theory, print the UPA illustration and see how it holds up on your next project. How many steps are you able to complete? Did you find yourself skipping steps, modifying them, or at times, not even able to pass start? The reason for bringing this up is that often, UX would use an approach that doesn't fit in well with the goals and objectives of the larger project team. For example, the following steps, taken directly from the UPA process map, are steps that are often excluded or heavily modified in real-world, multi team project settings:

- Assembling a multidisciplinary team to ensure expertise
  - ◦ **Modified**: This step is often based on budget, leadership, and how far along in the process the project is and when UX joined. In a perfect world, the team is working together like The Knights of the Round Table, but in reality, there are often many chinks in the armor.

- Conducting field studies
  - **Excluded**: There is a Beach Boys song that begins with the line "Wouldn't it be nice". Well, I don't mean to sound jaded, but field studies, otherwise known as **ethnography**, is one of the most enjoyable aspects of doing UX work. It is an opportunity to meet customers/users up close and personal and experience the environments in which they live and work. It provides a UX practitioner with great research findings that inform an entire team. The problem is that ethnography is often one of the first things to be cut in terms of time and budget, usually because nobody outside of the UX team can fully understand its value.

- Performing usability studies
  - **Excluded/Modified**: This is excluded or modified, depending on the project, the budget, and stakeholder goals. Traditionally, when UX maturity is at its lowest, usability studies are requested very late in the design and development process. By this time, most of the work has been completed and requirements have been set. Any usability issues reported by the UX team at this late stage is either problems the team already knew about or bad enough to scare them into ignoring it altogether for fear of going over budget to fix it and the risk of missing deadlines.

- Working closely with a delivery team
  - **Modified**: As stated earlier, we all want to be collaborators, and many will say they are. However, when developers get to work and project managers set their timelines for delivery, working with UX in an environment of low maturity can create headaches for the rest of the team. In these situations, the best a UX team can hope for is looking at what the developers coded, and providing some recommendations for improvements where needed. When or if they are implemented is another story.

- Monitoring the success of your work after launch
  - **Excluded**: Let's say that UX is able to do all of the things in the UPA process map, including the items mentioned in the previous bullets. Another issue that UX faces, is what happens after the product launches. When UX is brought in as a helper instead of a leader, monitoring our work and its subsequent success or failure is often someone else's responsibility.

Remember that in a team setting, as important as these steps may be to a UX practitioner, they are not as important to everyone else on the project team, including stakeholders. Pushing the issue can place UX in the precarious position of becoming a "nice to have" rather than a "must have". The truth is that while UX is a highly sought-after skill and ever present in more and more companies, it is still wildly misunderstood and highly undervalued by those who utilize it. What's more is that while the challenges UX faces are real, it is also true that much of the blame falls not on those who misunderstand its value, but on those who continue to perpetrate the problem.

The misunderstanding of UX

Another well-known UX process model is *The Elements of User Experience*, or the *Garrett Model*, named after its creator, Jesse James Garrett. Garrett's model, seen in the following image, depicts another well-organized and relatively straightforward approach to UX design:

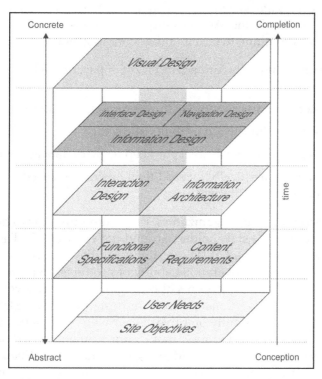

Source: https://efr0702.files.wordpress.com/2010/10/ux-elements-jjgarett.jpg

Viewed from the bottom up, Garret's model represents the steps and activities of a thorough, thoughtful, and consistent UX process, from *user needs* and *site objectives* to *visual design*. Like the UPA model, the Garrett model is easy to follow. It also poses the same challenge of UX wanting to do a lot of work up front while other project team members are doing their work. The reality is that not enough time or collaborative spirit exists to allow this to happen on a regular basis.

As a professional UX practitioner for over 10 years, I have experienced the frustration of trying to engage project teams and stakeholders to explain the value of UX and to prove its value. The problem, I came to understand, is that reaching this goal requires a totally different approach, one that those in our field don't often take, but need to if we are going to truly make a difference and become the leaders we were meant to be.

A different kind of UX approach

There is a well-known saying that states, *Insanity is doing something over and over again and expecting different results.* When we look at how UX has evolved over time, this definition hits too close to home. As an example, here are some common challenges that UX professionals continue to face in today's organizations:

- UX is not independently funded and is often part of the IT group or some other department
- UX will often modify its methods to accommodate rather than lead
- UX still focuses primarily on usability studies
- UX does not own, measure, track, or keep up with data and analytics
- UX is often more artistically focused than business focused (qualitative over quantitative)

Working as UX lead for a large organization, I was flummoxed as to how to better engage the company's stakeholders around the value of UX. The narrow understanding the company had of UX—usability studies, wireframes, reporting on heuristics, determining the overall likeability of products—was not improving our standing and doing nothing in terms of raising our maturity level as a team and as a practice. When we engaged on a project, our design work was strong, but we were still not engaging consistently on projects, nor were we in a position to track the success of our work, or continuously make improvements based on data and analytics. In essence, our UX team provided a specific function. When this function was completed, we disengaged, either on our own volition or as a result of the project team informing us that while our services were appreciated, we would no longer be needed at this time.

I came to refer to this process as the "front-door" approach, where engaging with teams meant asking permission to do our "specialized" work. Realizing that this approach was a long-term dead end, and one I had seen and experienced often in other companies as well, I started looking for another way.

What I found and developed was a way to close the "front door" and take a more strategic "back-door" approach—one that was much less conspicuous and ultimately proved to be far more influential. This new approach also provided stakeholders with an understanding of UX that they could identify with. The approach is so simple, in fact, that you can begin implementing it the moment you finish reading this chapter.

This is the approach, in three layers:

- Enterprise UX
- The business language of UX
- UX maturity milestones

Enterprise UX

Enterprise UX is a big topic and one that I won't get into it too broadly here. However, the simplest explanation is one I have mentioned numerous times throughout this book and is an approach to usability that focuses on three main areas:

- **Efficiency** (that is, time is money): This refers to designing solutions that allows data and content to be clearly, quickly, and consistently presented and understood, while ensuring that customers/users can complete their objectives in the same manner. Demonstrating our success in hard numbers is something stakeholders can understand and want to see in our work. An example of efficiency could be the time it takes to complete specific software/website/app related tasks versus the quality of the resulting output.

- **Effectiveness**: This refers to the degree to which customers/users are successfully using your design solutions and getting work done accurately and free of errors. We can also measure effectiveness using a variety of business metrics that we will look at later in this chapter. An example of effectiveness could be measuring the accuracy of tasks completed against the quality of the outcome versus the number of errors the user made in the process.

- **Satisfaction**: This refers to how quickly and how often your customers/users adopt your design solutions, how often do they continue using and engaging with your design, their comfort level in using it, and how much they trust that the design will consistently perform to their satisfaction. You can also measure satisfaction with regards to how happy your stakeholders are with your design, and by the increase in a stakeholder's understanding of the value that UX can deliver.

It is important to note that Enterprise UX was designed as an internally focused, employee approach to usability. This is also a topic that can fill an entire book of its own. Nevertheless, the strategy throughout the rest of the chapter will provide the essential elements you need to know to get started using this approach immediately.

 I have included resources in *Chapter 8, Final Thoughts and Additional Resources*, pertaining to Enterprise UX that will provide ample material to learn much more.

The business of UX

The next layer and the next important aspect of UX maturity is that of the business layer or business approach to UX. Remember, no matter what project you are working on, there will always be a stakeholder behind it with business needs, goals and objectives pertaining to it. This will be the case whether you work as an independent contractor, for a Fortune 500 company, or anywhere in between. At the end of the day, every project and idea has business needs, and as UX practitioners, it is our number one goal to know what those are and to be able to prove that we were successful. It is such an important priority that if I were using the Garrett model as an example, this layer would be the very first step in the process.

The reason this layer is so important is because it provides UX with the number one element needed to reach the highest level of UX maturity: business knowledge.

The first step is to find a project or problem to focus on. The key word here is *find*. Remember, using a "back-door" approach to UX means no longer waiting for projects to come your way. To move up the maturity ladder UX needs to lead.

With a back-door approach, projects can come from many places. You can begin by inviting stakeholders, i.e. decision makers and those accountable within their department for improving efficiency, effectiveness and satisfaction, to a meeting. Frame the meeting so that you grab their attention using language they understand. For example, here is an approach you could take, taken from an actual e-mail created for this very purpose:

> *Hi (stakeholder name)*
>
> *My name is (your name). I am working on a pilot project in the UX department and was wondering if I could have a few minutes of your time to tell you more about it and see if you would be interested in participating.*
>
> *Please let me know your availability and I will schedule a half hour to discuss.*
>
> *Regards,*
> *(Your name here)*

Once you get a response, here are three key questions to ask at the meeting:

- Tell me about some of the problems you may be having with your current application(s) that you would like to improve.

- If they provide you with some problems to solve, follow up by asking why it is a problem and how they know? Do not be afraid to pursue this line of questioning until you have answers that help you to fully understand the problem from their perspective. Remember that for UX to mature, you need to be more than an order taker. If a stakeholder tells you to stop asking questions and just go design what they are asking you for, be prepared to forever wallow in the morass of low UX maturity.

- Next ask: How does solving this problem fit into your department or team's overarching business objectives and the overall strategy for the company?

Remember that these are key questions, and their answers are vital to knowing what you are going to design. The answers will also provide you with some of the data you will need to know what you will be measuring as you create your designs.

The following are the three categories to focus on:

- **Financial**: How will your design achieve strategic and tactical goals?

- **Operational**: How will your design improve business processes?

- **Human**: How will your design affect the end user's experience?

Financial metrics

Financial goals generally fall into two basic categories:

- **Tactical**: Decreasing costs
- **Strategic**: Increasing profits

Choosing between them will depend on the nature of the project and also how visible the results are. For example, if you are asked to make design improvements to an internal software application, you can focus on the time it takes users to complete specific tasks, the average salary of employees who use the application, how much they make per hour, and how much the company can save if you can shorten time on task through improved design.

The only problem with this is that while it sounds great and can entice stakeholders with large-looking savings, you will also need to prove it. In some cases, this can be harder to do. How would you be able to prove, for example, that your design improvements did, in fact, increase efficiency and how can you accurately calculate that number? Raising the UX maturity level is going to take something more concrete and more visible.

Here are some **tactical** measurements to consider:

- Decreasing development time and costs
- Decreasing support costs
- Decreasing training costs
- Decreasing the burden on IT using better designed software
- Decreasing IT costs by lessening the need for help desk support and fixing usability issues
- Increasing user satisfaction

A **strategic** approach to measuring usability requires provable deliverables as well. Some of them are:

- Increasing the response time of customer support to our customers/users, whether by phone, e-mail, or chat
- Increasing user adoption, that is, the number of people who sign up or purchase a product
- Raising customer satisfaction scores
- Increasing overall company revenue
- Decreasing user's behavior of abandoning one company for a competitor

Let's look at a case study to get a clearer understanding of how to measure financial outcomes that really grab the attention of your stakeholder.

Case study: Strategic e-mail marketing campaign

The following case study details a metric driven UX approach that increased the number of new sales leads via an online lead-generation marketing form.

Initial problem (as outlined by the stakeholder)

An online marketing campaign was failing to generate a desirable number of new customer leads. In addition, people who submitted the online form were misunderstanding its purpose, using it instead as a way to ask general questions, rather than its intended purpose of inquiring about the company's products and services.

My approach

An initial review of the marketing campaign showed a poor approach to experience design, most glaringly, the content was missing a clear, specific call to action and the lead-generating submission form was "below the fold" — meaning it was unable to be seen without scrolling. Next, I asked for historical data to identify the metrics we would use as our baseline.

We chose the following metrics as our baseline to measure:

- Increase click conversion
- Increase web leads
- Increase phone leads
- Increase the total number of leads who became new customers
- Increase income generated from campaign design improvements

My process

The design process kicked off with a brainstorming session to create new call to action messaging, we then added some additional graphics and moved the web form higher up on the page to avoid scrolling. We created two versions of this design, with the second displaying a vertical web form in the right-hand column just to see if there was a difference in user response. Our test plan consisted of releasing one of the new designs, along with the current one and using a testing method called **A/B** or **split testing**, the end user would see either the current form, which we called **Baseline**, and one of the new forms, which we called **Design A** and **Design B**, respectively.

Results

The results of our test were as follows: **Design A** increased click conversion by 103 percent, web leads by 111 percent, and phone leads by 86 percent, with **Design B** not far behind:

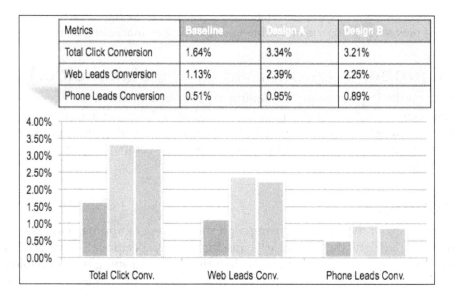

Metrics	Baseline	Design A	Design B
Total Click Conversion	1.64%	3.34%	3.21%
Web Leads Conversion	1.13%	2.39%	2.25%
Phone Leads Conversion	0.51%	0.95%	0.89%

As for increased business income, at the time of writing this book, the total number of leads that purchased products as well as the total increase in revenue was still unknown. The stakeholder's feedback, however, was promising, saying that they had never seen such a dramatic increase in conversion rates with any of their previous campaigns.

Operational metrics

This next category focuses on metrics to improve business processes, for example, by determining the usability of vendor software prior to purchase, informing the decision-making process, as well as focusing on employee-/customer-/user-facing software applications in order to improve user efficiency and effectiveness.

An example of the value of operational metrics and UX was proven in 2013 when makeup giant, Avon Products, Inc., decided against spending $125 million to overhaul their mobile iPad portal after an initial rollout proved so difficult to use that many of their sales reps quit as a result. — *Avon to Halt Rollout of New Order Management System, Drew Fitzgerald, Dec. 11, 2013,* http://www.wsj.com

Additional metrics for measuring operational improvements through UX include:

- Decreasing the number of user-related incidents due to poor design
- Improving ease of use to decrease the number of calls to customer support
- Identifying and improving potential interface issues before the product is launched to lower the costs associated with rework
- Increasing productivity of employees in their day-to-day activities

Case study: employee operational effectiveness

The following case study details an operational UX approach that improved stakeholder and employee effectiveness by implementing minor changes to an existing intranet landing page.

Initial problem (as outlined by the stakeholder)

A new data-intensive website was launched to provide sales reps with detailed customer sales data. According to the stakeholder of the project, the site was not being used as often as he would have liked. UX was asked to help improve the "look and feel" of the landing page to help resolve the issue.

My approach

My initial review of the landing page revealed a design that looked quite usable. Organizationally, it was easy to navigate and easy to locate important information. Nevertheless, we scheduled a number of user interviews to learn more and to satisfy my hypothesis that the design of the page was not the problem. After about a half dozen conversations with a mix of user types, we settled on the conclusion that the problem was not the design, but that most of the intended users were unaware that this page existed! I regrouped with the stakeholder for an in-depth conversation to identify some worthwhile metrics.

The result of this conversation identified some baseline measurements, which we would design to and later track to validate my assumptions. They were as follows:

- Increase the total number of unsolicited visits to the website from current users
- Increase the total number of unsolicited visits from new users
- Decrease the time the stakeholder was spending in informing potential users about the website.

My process

To create greater awareness of the website meant first understanding how users were finding it currently. The answer was via a link, buried deep within the navigation on an intranet portal. This made finding the website virtually impossible, unless the user was specifically looking for it and also knew where to look.

Pulling the link out of the drop-down menu and placing it in a more visible area on the intranet home page, along with a clear call to action, was all that was needed — at least that was the assumption. The last item to consider was the strict design style guidelines, dictated by a team elsewhere in the company who owned the intranet site and who were weary of "outsiders" making any changes. Following our design-improvements, we then tested our new design, which we again called **Design A,** with actual users in real-time.

Results

Following the launch of **Design A**, we saw the following improvements: increased total clicks by 166 percent, increased unique clicks by 275 percent, and reduced awareness/education time by 68 percent. Using a measurable approach to UX, we avoided the cost and time associated with redesigning a webpage, reduced employee waste and increased employee effectiveness and productivity by making a slight change to the location of a link on an existing landing page. The results of the test were as follows:

Metrics	Baseline	Design A
Total clicks from Intranet Site*	10%	26.6%
Unique clicks from Intranet Site	0.8%	3%
Awareness/Education Time**	10%	3.125%

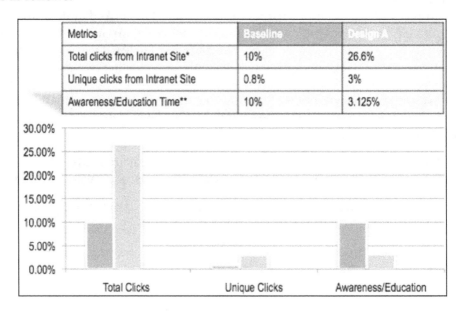

*Based on 1500 current total users of the new website

**Based on average time (approx 15 hrs/month) spent informing/reminding sales reps about the new website, updates, new data, and so on.

When you tap into the true value of UX, you literally help stakeholders make money, save time, and in the process, transform their understanding of the true value of UX.

Human metrics

The third category for measurable improvement is, of course, focused on human effectiveness and how your design affects the end user's experience overall.

Case study – improving user satisfaction and understanding

The following case study defined a measurable human approach to improving the user's experience and satisfaction of another internal website; further proving and ultimately clarifying the value of good UX design to the stakeholder.

Initial problem (as outlined by the stakeholder)

An existing risk-management website portal was failing with its intended users. The site was originally designed as a one-stop destination to educate and inform employees about company-related security risks and compliance standards as well as how to minimize and avoid them. Although the site was filled with important information, users were not engaging in the numbers the risk team had hoped. UX was asked to help generate ideas to improve this.

My approach

My initial review of the risk-management portal showed a poor approach to information architecture. Content was plentiful, but it was difficult to find, and search functionality was non-existent. When a user found valuable information, it was presented in multi-paged, hard-to-read legalese that required assistance or avoidance of the portal altogether.

Following some initial research to understand more about risk management and current usage, the stakeholder and I agreed to avoid the monumental task of redesigning the portal's information architecture and decided, instead, to focus on smaller, incremental changes. As a result, the following baseline metrics were chosen to measure and track:

- Decrease the need to assist users in finding content on the site
- Increase understandability of the portals content
- Increase the total number of visitors to the site

My process

The first improvement made was adding the search functionality. This required a close partnership with the development team to understand technology challenges with regard to implementation. We then determined the size of the effort to improve the site's overall content. Selecting a handful of popular security-related documents — ones that users asked most often about and ones they were most often noncompliant with — we gathered a team of subject matter experts to rewrite and shorten the content to a single page where possible, improve key word tagging, and incorporate other techniques to improve search results.

We then created a working prototype of the current site, including placement of a very conspicuous search input form field. Finally, we developed a number of user scenarios to subtly nudge our test users to the desired location for our test. We solicited a large number of user types (30) for in-person testing based of their past level of assistance needed and others who found content on the current site difficult to comprehend. We placed the participants into three groups of 10 and conducted an in-person, moderated study to determine the overall experience and satisfaction using the improved design.

Results

The results of our study showed a 100 percent decrease, with regards to the amount of assistance needed to find specific content. Our design improvements also showed an increase in the overall understandability of the improved content from 0 to 100 percent. With regards to the third metric, *increasing total number of visitors*, we were unable to sufficiently test this during our controlled study. However, the positive response we received from our test users gave us a relative baseline percentage to test against when the newly enhanced site became more widely distributed.

As for the business results of this project, although we were heavily focused on the human experience, we anticipated an increase in overall usage. This in turn would decrease company-wide security risk and lower company risk. This might not sound like much, but it is music to a business-minded executive's ears.

One more thing...

The case studies shared in this chapter detailed projects in which stakeholders asked UX for assistance with specific problems. However, this approach is not just reserved for when someone comes to you for help. One of the most exciting aspects of this business-focused approach to UX is that you can use it to find opportunities more easily than ever before.

Here are some steps to get you started:

- Begin by researching areas within your company or other companies that interest you, such as the company's customer-service team or a software application used by the sales team or some other group.

- Think about the stakeholders/clients you have worked with in the past. What business improvements can you identify for them that would provide value if they were improved?

- Ask these same stakeholders to share with you the problems or pain points they are currently experiencing, letting them know that working with UX can improve business results relatively quickly.

- Look at Web and mobile apps that your company produces and use your business-focused UX approach to find opportunities for improvement. Remember, stakeholders don't care how great of a designer you are. What they want to know is what you can do for *them*!

- Explain how you plan to test your work and how you will track it after it launches to make sure that the results you promised come to pass. Stick with it until it does and then continue monitoring it with future improvements in mind.

Keep in mind too that many measurable business improvements can be accomplished easily and relatively quickly. It is also important to remember that good design is not about how it looks as much as it is about how it acts and what it provides in terms of effectiveness, efficiency and satisfaction. Remember that even ugly websites (Google, Ebay, Craigslist. W3C, Wikipedia) can be hugely successful, not because of how they look, but because of how they work, their well-designed IA, and the value they provide to customers, users, and stakeholders.

The UX maturity map

Once you put this approach into place and begin seeing stakeholder engagement rapidly improve, you will want to monitor your progress along the way to know where you are and where you want to be. The following UX maturity diagram will help guide you through this:

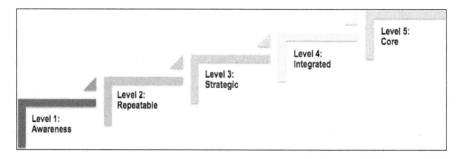

Let's review each maturity level:

Level 1 – Awareness

At this stage, UX regularly seeks opportunities to pilot small, measurable user-facing projects to demonstrate business-focused improvements. Projects at this maturity level are acquired or created through independent research or as a result of stakeholders/ clients requesting UX assistance and expertise.

Level 2 – Repeatable

At this stage, UX has completed a number of successful, business-oriented, metric-driven projects and has developed a repeatable process to deliver customer-/user-facing business improvements to stakeholders/clients consistently across the company.

Level 3 – Strategic

At this stage, UX is ready to take on large customer-/user-facing projects and may have done so already. Business improvements using metric driven UX design techniques are socialized across the company, and stakeholders/clients are excited and eager to share their success with a larger audience. Leaders at the executive level are beginning to take notice of UX as being a strategic, untapped value stream.

Level 4 – Integrated

At this stage, the company's understanding of UX has been transformed from a team that does usability studies to one that provides undeniable, provable, measurable business results. UX participates in high-level strategic planning meetings and has gained the full support of executive leadership (CIO, CTO, CEO). UX has now gained enough influence to become its own independent department within the company, with an independent source of funding and UX leadership at the executive level.

Level 5 – Core

At this stage, UX is as integral to the company or client as IT, marketing, and customer experience (CX), along with a budget and team to match. All customer-/user-facing decisions, from innovation to projects to software purchases involve UX at the earliest stages and at the leadership level.

Summary

In this chapter we looked at the problem with UX maturity as well as an approach to raising it, both as an individual UX practitioner and within a company. We looked at case studies using this approach and how the results it produced dramatically changed the perception of UX value with stakeholders. Lastly, we looked at a maturity model to use to gauge your UX maturity success as you begin to use this approach on real world projects where your clients and stakeholders want to see measurable, provable results.

Today, too many UX practitioners and teams face the challenge of proving the true value of UX design work to stakeholders. It is a problem that will continue so long as we continue speaking to them in the language of design. While design language is necessary for the success of our customers and end users who will interact with it, we must also remember that stakeholders speak the language of business. It is a language we must also be fluent in to more effectively connect with them to prove the value of UX on their terms.

If doing the same thing again and again and expecting a different result is the definition of insanity then it is time to change our approach in order to help stakeholders to understand its true value of UX. Following the approach presented in this chapter you can deliver that result.

As UX practitioners, our job is to listen to our customers and walk in their shoes to solve their specific problems. Stakeholders are no different and just as important as any of your customers and end users. They are also key to your ongoing success and longevity as a UX practitioner because without them, there are no new products and no new projects. Keep that in mind every single day when you go to work.

7
UX Tools

"We become what we behold. We shape our tools, and thereafter our tools shape us."

– Marshall McLuhan

Writing about UX tools in a book can sometimes be a wasted effort. Technology changes so quickly that what was new today becomes obsolete or out of date by the time the book is published. Add to this an ever-growing array of UX job titles — designer, architect, ethnographer, researcher, engineer — and an increasing array of tools, and it becomes hard to know which tools to use and how to choose. That said, to provide you with useful information that won't go out of style, let's look at some of the UX tools that never do.

In this chapter, we will cover:

- The tools of the UX trade
- How to get the most out of your tools
- Why the most useful tools never go out of style

Tools of the UX trade

Use Google to search for UX tools, and you'll find results with terms such as A/B or split testing, accessibility, wireframing, mapping, user and usability testing, prototyping, evaluation, mobile app testing, analytics, and so on. Now, use Google to search for the term "choosing the right UX tools" or "the best UX tools," and an equally large number of resources appear. With so many options and so little time to learn them all, what's a UX practitioner to do?

While I use tools that are personal favorites, there are many more that I haven't tried. Once you begin trying them, you will probably find that a lot of them do pretty much the same thing. One wireframing tool is often as good as another, save perhaps for some additional features such as ease of use, price, and so on. Tools for technology are really not much different than tools for any other field. If I am building a bookshelf, any hammer, saw, and drill would work, but there is also nothing like using better made, higher quality tools when you can.

UX-related tools are not much different. A card sort can still be done by hand even though UserZoom exists, and simple wireframes can still be drawn by hand instead of using Axure or Balsamiq. Of course, tools for technology were created to make the work that used to be done by hand easier, faster, more efficient, and often more effective. Having tools like Photoshop, Visio, Balsamiq, Axure, and others as alternatives to doing that work by hand is great, but then again, knowing how to do those things that software applications can do more quickly and easily is actually just as important. For example, you don't need Balsamiq or Axure to draw a wireframe when a napkin and a pen will do, and you don't need Visio to create a site map or to map out your site or application's information architecture, but it sure makes life easier when you do. The bottom line with UX tools is simple: don't worry about how many tools there are and knowing them all. Instead, just focus on the following:

- Learn the tools your company and team uses, if it creates collaboration and design consistency
- Use only the tools you really need to get the job done, then spend the rest of your time improving your skills as an information architect, designer, researcher, and business focused practitioner
- If you are new to UX related tools, start with the ones easiest to learn, like Balsamiq for wireframes and OmniGraffle
- As for visual design, save yourself the time of learning complex graphic applications and partner with a visual designer whose job it is to know these tools at an expert level

Your job and your role as a UX practitioner is not to know every tool. It is to know only the ones that help you get the job done when you need them. If you are unfamiliar with any of these tools and just want to explore, go for it. Most provide trial periods that allow you to do that risk free.

What follows is what I consider to be some of the most useful tools in the UX practitioner's toolbox. You might not use them right away, or at all, however, knowing about them and why they are used can make a noticeable difference in your work.

Personas

"Design is really an act of communication, which means having a deep understanding of the person with whom the designer is communicating."

– Donald A. Norman, The Design of Everyday Things

Personas are defined as "fictional characters created to represent the different user types that might use a site, brand, or product in a similar way. " — `https://en.wikipedia.org/wiki/Persona_(user_experience)`.

If you have never seen a persona, it looks like this:

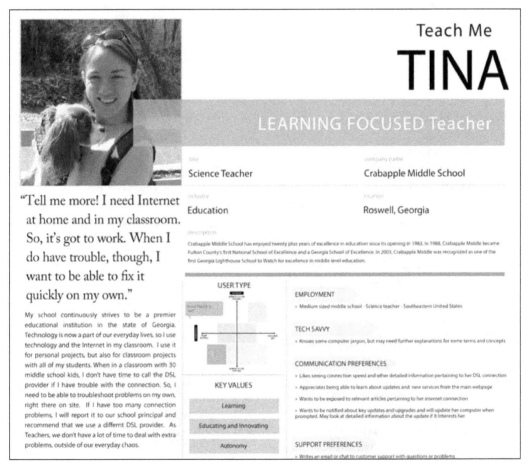

Source: `http://uxmag.com/sites/default/files/uploads/oconnorpersonas/samplepersona.png`

Basically, personas are a one-page depiction of a specific customer/user type that is supposed to tell us all we need to know about that demographic. The value of personas is two fold:

- To remind individuals and teams who interact with data more often than with real customers/users that their work has real-world consequences
- To create empathy and to remind designers not to base their work on their own personal desires, but on the needs and desires of their customers/users, the ones who will actually be using it

I am not a fan of personas. They are one-dimensional, expensive to create, and feed into the "faster horse" myth, especially at the executive level. They can create the false impression that we know everything about our customers/users and we no longer need to engage with them. Of course, there are two sides to this debate, and I encourage you to decide for yourself if you want to use them or not. Remember, though, that in a mature UX environment, there is never a substitute for real-life connection and interaction.

If you do want to use personas, I highly recommend creating them from real feedback you get after intensive research and ethnography studies of your actual customers/users. This means too that you will probably have a number of personas, because everyone is different and each has specific needs that will continue to change and evolve. As a result, be prepared to update your personas on a regular basis. If you find however, that you are unable or unwilling to do the research necessary to create your own personas created by a hired vendor that specializes in personas or ones created by another department within your company will not be very helpful.

The human persona

Although I am not a fan of personas, there *is* one persona type that I *would* consider when ethnography and research of your customers/users is not in the budget. I call it the human persona.

The human persona is non-specifc, and as a result acts as a strong reminder of the most important user type there is: the human user. When we look back, throughout this book, we would find examples that touch upon the human experience rather than "Teach Me Tina's" experience in the previous example. Sure, "Tina" may have certain needs and desires, but then again, good design should not be geared to any one person or personality type. Good design should reach any type. Whether everyone uses it is not the point.

Leave that to the marketing department. Good UX is about design that connects people, draws people in, engages and allows for easy interaction, provides for efficiency and effectiveness, and leaves the user with some sense of satisfaction. The human persona can help get you a little bit closer to that.

Now, I am not saying everyone is the same, nor am I suggesting that the human persona is all we need. What I am suggesting, however, is that if we are truly doing our due diligence as practitioners in a mature, customer-/user-focused way, then we should not have time to rely on one-dimensional creations, because we are too busy talking with and learning from the three-dimensional ones.

Ethnography

If you were to look for a definition of the exact opposite of personas, you would look no further than **Ethnography**. Ethnography literally means immersion, observation, and engagement with real people in their natural element. For a UX practitioner, this could mean visiting a doctor in rural Kansas to learn how they use a suite of applications in their office and then visiting a doctor at Rush University Medical Center in Chicago, IL using the same applications. You could then board a plane to Brazil for yet another perspective. The enlightenment brought about by ethnography and ethnographic research is what every UX researcher and practitioner aspires to, but very seldom accomplishes on a consistent basis. Ethnography has become such a rare occurrence in the working world of UX that an acronym was created to remind people to do it. "GOOB" or "Get Out Of (the) Building" is a term coined by Stanford professor and entrepreneur Steve Blank. He wanted to encourage project/product team members to get out of the office and put their work in front of real users to see the results of their work first hand, rather than assume they already knew what customers/users wanted. Ethnography is a much larger topic than I am going to talk about here, but I encourage you to use Google to look for it and start digging in.

Human centered design

One of the outcroppings of ethnography is **Human Centered Design** (HCD), an approach to problem solving that begins and ends with understanding the needs of real people and designing solutions to match. While there are many similarities between **UX Design** (UXD) and HCD, HCD design does not move forward without immersion into the lives and experience of those for whom you design.

To learn more about HCD, I highly recommend that you download and read *The Field Guide to Human-Centered Design*, a monumental achievement of a document by IDEO that guides you step-by-step through the process of "solving problems like a designer."

> *"The Field Guide has everything you need to understand the people you're designing for, to have more effective brainstorms, to prototype your ideas, and to ultimately arrive at more creative solutions."*
>
> *– IDEO.org*

 To download a free copy of *The Field Guide to Human-Centered Design*, go to `http://www.designkit.org/human-centered-design`.

Journey maps

Journey maps are a literal mapping of an end-to-end experience of a customer/user. It can also map simultaneously what happens on the back end of the journey. For example, you could map all of the internal systems and internal touch points that happen during a single customer/user engagement or map every interaction of an application and its outcome. The value of such a tool is that it enables UX practitioners to see every step, be it a transaction, an interaction, communication, and so on, with a bird's eye view. It also allows you to see **pain points**, which are areas in your design that are causing user confusion, as well as **moments of truth**, which are the moments when your designs provide either a good or bad impression. This can happen so quickly that often the only way to see them is to visualize every step of the journey.

To give you an example of a journey map, here is a close up section of one:

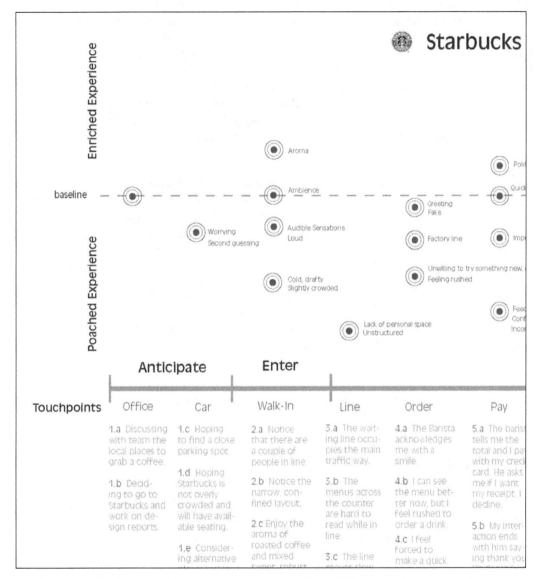

https://bschrum.files.wordpress.com/2013/03/experiencemap11.jpg

The example in the preceding image is a journey map created for Starbucks to visualize each step in a customer's journey, from simply having the idea for coffee to enjoying it after they purchased and everything in between. The top portion of the map shows a visual representation of each step, separated by a middle point called, in this example, the **baseline**. Touch points above the line are seen as enriched experiences for the customer, while touch points below the line are considered to be negative and possible pain points and moments of truth for the company to take notice of and improve upon, provided they see a reason for doing so. Creating a journey map is also a great way to provide stakeholders with a visual representation of an entire customer/user journey as well as to point out areas of opportunity to improve some kind of business metric, be it monetary or otherwise.

Please note too that journey maps come in all shapes and sizes, and there is no set look to them. You are not really constrained visually, however you will want to create some kind of baseline to delineate when an experience is positive and negative as well as making room to capture whatever notes and observations you want to make.

Journey maps are a great tool because they help identify and zero in on problem areas, whether it's a bottleneck causing a slowdown in an interface design or perhaps it's something larger, like a backend system in need of updating. Uncovering problem areas, pain points, and moments for improvements using journey maps provides UX practitioners with a more holistic understanding of business/customer/ user relationships, interactions, and even entire ecosystems.

 For more information and examples of journey maps, enter the search term customer journey experience maps in Google.

Usability studies

Usability studies will put, perhaps the most well-known tool in the UX practitioner's toolbox, your design solutions to the test. Using an array of strategies, such as card sorting, and in-person and remote testing, these tools bring to the fore the importance of making sure that what is being delivered not only solves a problem, but that it does so easily and clearly for the end user.

The first and most important aspect to usability studies is to remember that this is an opportunity to engage and connect with customers/users in person, provided, of course, that you are performing in-person studies. If so, they are often best approached from a human rather than a scientific perspective.

Some UX practitioners will often create a script, which is essentially a document detailing every question they want to ask. While I am not discounting the approach, it is highly recommended that you moderate a usability study more like a conversation, rather than relying on something less flexible like a script. This also allows for better listening and more opportunities to think about what the test participant is actually saying, rather than waiting to ask the next question.

Also, if you are moderating a study, meaning you are leading it and guiding the test participants through it, it is recommended that you not be the one taking notes! Like a script, it is another distraction between you and your study participant be present. Ask a colleague to join you for note taking and any other duties that need to be performed during this crucial, limited time you have with the people who are going to share with you information that you cannot get anywhere else.

RITE usability testing

Now, you may be thinking: "well this sounds good, but what if I don't have the budget for a formal usability study?" It is a good question, because this is one of the challenges faced by many UX teams. Luckily, there is a tool for that as well.

Known as **Rapid Iterative Testing and Evaluation (RITE)**, this method of usability testing follows many of the same steps as a normal usability study:

- Criteria for testing is defined
- A population of users are identified and scheduled—either remotely, in-person and in groups, or one on one
- A measurement strategy is devised, and so on

What differs with RITE testing is the speed in which testing, iterating, and updating is done. Normally, issues uncovered during usability testing are fixed and improved after the test and, perhaps, tested again at a later time. The RITE method requires that any design problems discovered during a usability study be addressed the moment they appear and rapidly fixed, as soon as a better solution is determined. Sometimes, changes will be made after only one person has been tested and a problem identified. Following that, any improvements are tested with subsequent participants and so on until the team feels they have uncovered and fixed any and all potential usability problems.

Performing studies in this manner allows the UX researcher to do the required work, but in a much quicker way and usually without the luxury of a UX lab or some other controlled space. Unlike formal usability studies, RITE testing can be performed anywhere that the user has a computer, a mobile device, or any other method of interfacing and interacting with your design. Perhaps the biggest benefit of RITE testing is that it allows for usability studies on a smaller budget and within a much shorter timeframe. In today's professional work environment, time is often something we do not seem to ever have enough of.

 For more information on the RITE testing method, enter the search term `Rapid Iterative Testing and Evaluation` or `UX RITE testing` in Google.

Usability study reporting

Following the completion of your usability study, and after the notes and observations have been documented, the UX team will report their findings. Reports can take on many forms. Most often, they are PowerPoint presentations or multi-page Word documents detailing every scenario tested, screenshots, and the results of the test itself. Reporting can be a very valuable document for stakeholders to read and share with their colleagues. Reporting can also present the UX practitioner with a number of challenges that you should be aware of and avoid. Some of them are mentioned here:

- Failure to provide a high-level report summary to your stakeholders
- Reporting results about usability and user reactions to the design, but excluding the expected business value
- Providing too much detail and not enough substance
- Giving stakeholders more information than they want or need
- Trying to impress rather than inform
- Thinking that your stakeholders actually care about the usability report

Unless your stakeholders are usability practitioners or they had a part in designing the product you tested, they are less interested in the study and more interested in how your findings will affect their business goals and when you are going to fix any problems. This is the key to reaching a higher level of UX maturity, something we reviewed in detail in *Chapter 6, An Essential Strategy for UX Maturity*. Talking about UX with stakeholders is like a builder telling you how they are going to install your new kitchen cabinets.

Unless installing kitchen cabinets is of interest to you, you just expect them to get it done correctly. It is no different when working with stakeholders who want to trust that they can see the results of your work and share that success with *their boss*, who cares more about business results than anything else.

Visual design

If you recall the Garrett UX process model from *Chapter 6, An Essential Strategy for UX Maturity*, **visual design** is represented in the top most layer. Visual design is often referred to as providing the "look and feel" of a design or putting the "skin" on the wireframe "skeleton." It is also the time in the design process when the essential elements of the design—the wireframes, content, information architecture, usability testing, and so on should be complete. The reason is that any new changes or fixes after this stage will be costly to fix because the majority of the work has already been completed.

It is important to mention that while we have used the term *design* a lot, UX design and visual design are not the same. Each have their own processes and techniques and each are usually performed separately, usually after the UX design work has been completed. Nevertheless, UX practitioners are not exempt from visual design duties and may be required to handle those responsibilities from time to time. As we have seen, having an eye for design and recognizing good from bad is required knowledge for everyone involved. Knowing what to look for and how to communicate your ideas to those doing the work is just as important as if you were doing it yourself.

Cynefin

In addition to the popular UX tools, there are also those that, while perhaps lesser known, are still quite useful and good to know. Cynefin, pronounced [Kih-neh-vihn], is one of those tools. Cynefin is a framework developed by Welsh researcher and founder of Cognitive Edge, Dave Snowden. It is used to help teams identify project complexity and to inform the project-planning phase.

Cynefin is made up of four-quadrants, each identifying the various levels of complexity for any given problem, along with tips on how to solve it.

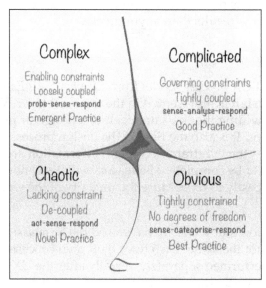

There is a fifth domain as well, but we will get to that in a moment. First, here is a brief explanation of the four main quadrants:

- **Complex**: In this domain, previous project experience may not apply. In the complex quadrant, research and experimentation are vital to success in problem solving. The types of problems encountered in the complex space are often solved through extensive research and brainstorming because solutions are not straightforward or easy. Do not cut corners when faced with complexity and avoid rushing to a solution too quickly. As we learned in *Chapter 2, Creative UX*, plan ahead and allow for the time to stay in open mode for your best work to come through. Any other approach in the complex space, and you may end up wasting time and money on the wrong solution.

- **Complicated**: In this domain, you have a general sense of what's needed and have perhaps seen and dealt with this type of problem before. Nevertheless, complicated problems still require a good deal of research and careful analysis to get it right. You will also need the help of others, specifically **subject matter experts (SMEs)**, to make sure you get clear answers to complicated questions. There is more risk associated with this domain as well. Move carefully, but knowingly.

- **Chaotic**: In this domain, normalcy takes a back seat to panic, as problems have gotten to the point where doing nothing is no longer an option. For example, imagine that your e-commerce site has a programming flaw that allows customers to purchase two items for the price of one. Alternatively, maybe, the system is overcharging or undercharging for an item. Problems like this force a team into the "triage" mode just to "stop the bleeding," so to speak. On the positive side, many chaotic problems are often easy to fix as long as the team is quick to identify the root causes of the problem and is decisive in taking action.

- **Obvious**: Problems found here are pretty straightforward and can often rely on best practices to solve it. You should still test and validate solutions in this quadrant if the problem warrants it. If not, you could move forward with a good degree of certainty and confidence that your solution will resolve the issue.

Earlier, I mentioned there was be a fifth domain. It's the area in the center, appropriately called "disorder." This center area is where you land when you don't clearly know which domain to choose. If you find yourself in disorder, it probably means you don't yet fully understand the problem. Using Cynefin, the goal is to always know which of the four visible quadrants is correct. This may require the help of a team to help you decide and to gain consensus before moving forward in order to ensure more informed decisions and more valuable and viable solutions.

Business model canvas

As was discussed in the previous chapter, proving the true value of UX requires that we speak to stakeholders using the language of business. Knowing about metrics and what to measure is key. However, there are also other considerations to think about. The business model canvas can help.

The business model canvas, or BMC, is described as:

> *"A strategic management and entrepreneurial tool…[that] allows you to describe, design, challenge, invent, and pivot your business model."*

> – http://www.businessmodelgeneration.com/canvas/bmc

The following image is an example of what the BMC tool looks like:

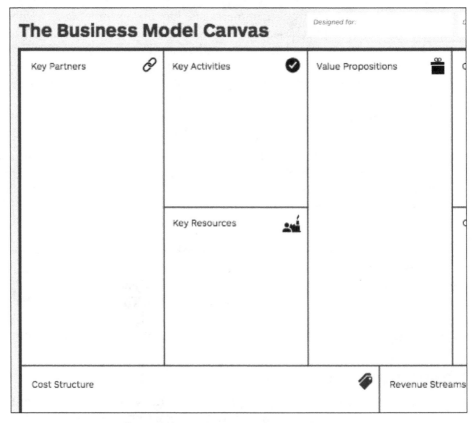

Source: www.businessmodelgeneration.com

As a business tool, the Canvas provides key objectives and areas of focus important to teams, such as identifying the right people, activities, value proposition, and other aspects important to stakeholders and the overall outcome of a project. Using the BMC is also pretty simple. You can begin by printing out a blank copy of the Canvas at businessmodelgeneration.com or generate one online at canvanizer. com or leanstack.com. Then, review the free tutorials provided and give it a try. Remember that you don't have to use every tool in your bag all the time, but knowing how to use the tools when you need them can make your job a lot easier.

Wireframes and prototyping

Another layer in the Garrett model, just before visual design, requires a set of tools you will be using quite often and may already be familiar with: wireframes and prototypes. Garrett refers to this layer as the "Skeleton Plane" because wireframes provide the grid work or the bones that we cover or "skin" with visual design.

Here is a basic example of what a wireframe might look like:

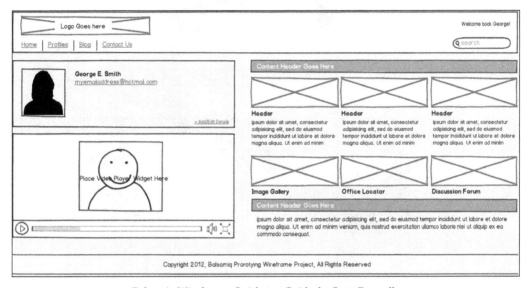

Balsamiq Wireframes Quickstart Guide, by Scott Faranello

As you can see, a wireframe presents a very rough, almost sketch-like appearance. This is intentional because we want to avoid any other visual distractions, like colors, fonts, images and so on. Wireframes also allow the designer to demonstrate how an idea will work at its most basic level, while allowing for any changes to the design to occur quickly and easily.

Once a design is reviewed and accepted as a workable solution, the next step is to put it in front of users to see if it lives up to the designer's expectations. For the designer, this means putting together a working model or prototype for users to try for themselves.

The prototype is an interactive version of your wireframe, where the user can interact with your design using any number of scenarios and performing any number of tasks. Prototyping can be accomplished in several ways — one way is to use paper to show transitions from screen to screen:

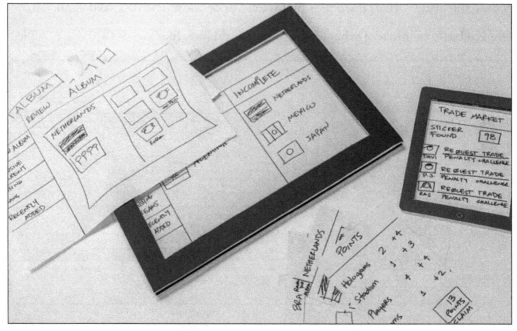

Source: http://desarrolloweb.dlsi.ua.es/cursos/2015/hci/images/screen-frame-02.jpg

Prototyping can also be accomplished using applications such as Balsamiq and Axure and with HTML-coded pages. Whichever method you choose, prototypes are the first time your ideas will be tested with real users and will help you gauge whether your intended design meets your user's expectations.

 If you would like to learn more about wireframes and how to use one of the best available tools for the job, pick up a copy of my book, *Balsamiq Wireframes Quickstart Guide,* from Packt's website or on Amazon.

A closing thought

There is a classic stage play and film of the same name called *Glengarry Glen Ross* in which the phrase **Always Be Closing** (**ABC**) was popularized and came to define the art of selling and salesmanship. Well, I will create a new phrase for UX right now: **Always Be Learning** (**ABL**).

Like any profession worth pursuing, there should always be something more to learn and something new to discover on a regular basis. UX provides a wellspring of learning, where almost daily new information comes along to challenge what we thought we knew and to provide us with a glimpse into what may be around the corner. With UX, there is no shortage of new ideas and when you discover them, it's in your best interest to understand and pursue them to the fullest extent. Some may be trends, while others may be fads. Nevertheles, like tools, it is always good to know about them and how to use them, because one day they may come in handy.

For example, here are some trends that keep popping up:

- Invisible design
- Consumerization of design
- Frictionless design
- Uniformity of design
- Advanced technologies (IoT)
- Generational expectations of technology

Google these terms, learn about them and maybe even find a use for them. As we have seen throughout this book, tools are always present, available and ready for use, provided you allow yourself to see them and learn from them. When you do, you will find that many of these tools were there all along. You just didn't know to look, or perhaps you were in the closed mode and simply couldn't see. Knowing the tools available to you and learning how to use them can make a big difference in how and what you create, but that is only half the story. Tools are useless unless you use them to create something new and perhaps something better. Where you go from there is up to you.

Summary

In this chapter we looked at the tools of the UX trade, how to get the most out of your tools and why the most useful tools never go out of style. Know your tools, find your favorites and then make room for all of your new and creative ideas that are sure to come.

8

Final Thoughts and Additional Resources

"Never put passion before principle. Even if win, you lose."

– Kesuke Miyagi

When I was originally asked to write a book about UX, it was intended as a practical guide to improve one's web design work. As I started writing and outlining the book, I quickly realized that it was impossible to talk about designing better without explaining why it mattered. As a skill and field, UX is more than tips and tricks. It is a lifelong pursuit of understanding what motivates different people and how to deliver that through design. UX is an art form that, like all other art forms, improves with some historical perspective and a deeper understanding of its connections to the larger world. Of course, it's possible to become a UX designer without making these connections, but that's a decision and a choice. For some, UX is a job. For others, it's a passionate pursuit of knowledge and history that brings us closer to embodying the work we deliver.

I hope that this book has brought you closer to the latter and that you are able to incorporate what you've learned into your work as a result. However, don't stop here. Many of the topics covered in this book by many sources that should be shared so that you can continue learning, exploring and growing as a UX minded practitioner.

In this final chapter, you will find resources for further learning, such as books, blogs, terms, websites, tools, and people to pursue.

Measuring UX

A listing of resources pertaining to measuring the true value of UX.

Metrics

The strategy and approach of measuring UX outlined in *Chapter 6, An Essential Strategy for UX Maturity* can truly drive UX success, understanding, maturity, and long-term success on a consistent basis. To effectively pursue this strategy requires that you not only use a measurable approach, but also know what to measure. Here are some examples of some of the types of metrics you can use. This is not a complete list. They are provided to get you thinking about metrics and about what can be measured. The choices are vast and limited only by your imagination and your understanding of the language of business.

Financial performance metrics:

- Percentage of IT expenditures to deliver new functionality
- Total spending reduced by business unit
- Total value creation from UX-enabled projects
- Percentage of decreased annual IT costs
- Differential in business case estimate and actual benefits
- Net present value delivered during payback period
- Actual versus planned ROI
- Percentage of target user population using the functionality delivered
- Share of IT training spent in a business unit
- Number of training hours per employee per quarter
- Dollars saved through process improvements
- Business hours lost due to avoidable activities
- Total value created

Operational performance metrics:

- Number of applications used by more than one line of business
- Average number of incidents per user per month
- Revenue loss from impaired end user productivity
- Number of high-impact incidents identified and prevented

User satisfaction metrics:

- Average end user satisfaction rating
- Average business executive satisfaction rating
- Help-desk satisfaction
- Business process improvements
- Contribution to corporate business strategy
- Help-desk tickets per user per month
- Business value creation
- Abandon call rate
- Perceived contribution to competitive advantage
- Adoption rate versus baseline

Books and articles

Here are some books and articles on measuring UX and business results:

- *Measuring the User Experience, Second Edition: Collecting, Analyzing, and Presenting Usability Metrics*, by William Albert, Thomas Tullis
- *Quantifying the User Experience: Practical Statistics for User Research*, by Jeff Sauro, James R Lewis
- *Cost-Justifying Usability, Second Edition: An Update for the Internet Age*, by Randolph G. Bias, Deborah J. Mayhew
- *A Strategic Approach to Metrics for User Experience*, Carl W. Turner, Ph.D., Journal of Usability Studies, Vol. 6, Issue 2, February 2011, pp. 52-59
- *Leveraging Business Value: How ROI Changes User Experience*, Sara Beckman, Janice Fraser, Scott Hirsch, Adaptive Path, 2004
- *How to Modernize User Experience*, by Leah Buley, Forrester Research, Inc., March 23, 2015
- *Quantifying Usability*, Jeff Sauro, Interactions, November/December, 2006

Google terms

Type these terms into Google for additional research and information on measuring UX:

- Measuring the user experience
- ROI of UX
- UX business impacts and ROI
- UX ROI metrics
- Calculating the ROI of UX

Online measurement tools

Here are some useful online tools to input measurable data:

- `softwareadvice.com/tco/`
- `humanfactors.com/coolstuff/roi.asp`
- `sapcampaigns.de/us/UX_Calculator/`
- `zendesk.com/customer-service-roi-calculator`

Enterprise UX

Books and articles about Enterprise UX:

- *UX for the Enterprise,* Jordan Koschei, alistapart.com, November 2014, `http://alistapart.com/article/ux-for-the-enterprise`
- *The User Experience of Enterprise Software Matters,* Paul J. Sherman, UX Matters.com, December, 2008, `http://www.uxmatters.com/mt/archives/2008/12/the-user-experience-of-enterprise-software-matters.php`
- *Enterprise UX, the Next Last Frontier,* Patrick Neeman, slideshare.net, `http://www.slideshare.net/usabilitycounts/enterprise-ux-the-next-last-frontier`
- *Rethinking Enterprise UX in the Age of Consumerization,* Michael Ashley, July, 2013, `https://uxmag.com/articles/rethinking-enterprise-ux-in-the-age-of-consumerization`

- *Stepping Up: UX in the Enterprise*, Anton Baturan, User Experience Magazine, 2015, `http://uxpamagazine.org/stepping-up/`

- *Intersection: How Enterprise Design Bridges the Gap between Business, Technology, and People*, Milan Guenther, 2012

UX-related websites

Here are some of the best websites to learn about and keep up with all things UX:

- `uxpin.com`
- `uxmatters.com`
- `smashingmagazine.com`
- `usabilitygeek.com`
- `uxbooth.com`
- `alistapart.com`
- `adaptivepath.com`
- `boxesandarrows.com`
- `lukew.com`
- `nngroup.com`
- `tandemseven.com`
- `usabilityprofessionals.org`
- `uxmag.com`
- `cognitive-edge.com`

UX-related books

Follow these links to find lists of recommended UX books:

- `uxdesign.cc/ux-books`
- `blog.careerfoundry.com/best-books-ux`

Mobile patterns

Links to great mobile designs and mobile design patterns:

- `androidpatterns.com`
- `androidux.com`
- `appreciateui.com`

- inspired-ui.com
- ios-patterns.com
- mobile-patterns.com
- mobiletuxedo.com
- pttrns.com
- ui-patterns.com
- uxarchive.com

Additional UX design tools

You want tools? Follows these links to find tons of them:

- uxdesign.cc/ux-tools
- uxmastery.com/resources/tools

People to follow

Go to Google and type in the names of the following UX minded people who have lived and continue to live in the open mode most of the time." Follow them on Twitter, read their books, find their articles and listen to what they have to say. You might find it was well worth your time.

- Chistopher Alexander
- Will Evans
- Jesse James Garrett
- Dave Snowden
- Donald A. Norman
- Dieter Rams
- Henry Ford
- Jeff Sauro
- John Shook
- Peter M. Senge
- Richard Saul Wurman
- Dr. Susan Weinschenk

Summary

There you have it: an approach to UX that I hope has provided you with some food for thought, some inspiration, a few new ideas to try when you return to work and a more mature approach and strategy for providing stakeholders, customers, and users with the best possible experience and the greatest value.

UX is much more than visual design, usability studies, and look and feel. These are important, but UX design is more effective and meaningful when we incorporate mindset, creativity, open-mode thinking, good IA, effective process, design from a wider perspective, knowledge of your tools, and continuing to learn on a daily basis. These are all integral to your growth and maturity as a UX practitioner and the foundation for all that you will design, create, and build going forward.

Thank you for taking this journey with me. It was a life-changing experience to write this book. I hope you have enjoyed it, learned from it, and widened your perspective enough to begin noticing significant improvements in your work right away. If so, let me know. I wish you the best in all your UX pursuits and endeavors, and my sincerest thanks for your interest and attention.

Index

A

Always Be Closing (ABC) 195
Always Be Learning (ABL) 195
Apple store
  floor plan 108

B

baseline 186
boundaries
  about 129, 130
  safe boundaries 132, 133
  testing 131
business-focused approach
  steps 175
business model canvas (BMC)
  reference link 191
business, UX
  about 166-175
  financial metrics 168
  human metrics 173
  operational metrics 170

C

Central Park
  reference link 128
change
  consequences 92
  designing for 90, 91
closed mode
  about 24
  combining, with open mode 26, 27
  using 25, 26

consistency 154
contrast 149
creativity conditions
  10,000 hour rule 32-34
  about 29
  agreement 30, 36
  confidence 30-35
  humor 30
  play 35, 36
  space 30, 31
  time 30, 31
creativity modes
  closed mode 24
  open mode 24
Customer-Focused Innovation (CFI) 18
Cynefin
  about 189
  chaotic 191
  complex 190
  complicated 190
  obvious 191

D

data-driven design 14
design 41
design thinking
  about 16
  business (viability) 17
  human values (usability, desirability) 17
  technology (feasibility) 17
Dieter Rams designs
  URL 60
Dvorak keyboard 52

originality 58-60
safety 71, 73
three-second rule used 67-69
understandability 65-67
understandability, failure 69, 70
usefulness 60-63
valuable 70
good IA
about 80
examples 110
gradient-based transitions
Fade 152
Flip 152
Flow 152
Pop 152
Slide 152
Slidedown 152
Slidefade 152
Slideup 152
Turn 152
gradients
about 151
gradient-based transitions 152

H

Hamburger Icon Test
reference link 132
hierarchical taxonomy 87, 88
Human Centered Design (HCD) 183
human factors
reference 3
human metrics
approach 173
initial problem 173
process 174
results 174
user satisfaction, improving 173
human persona 182

I

IA
about 79
four Cs 80-83
success, gauging 99, 100

IA, of cities
about 92
fractal loading 93, 94
improved design solution 51
information architecture. *See* **IA**
Information Technology (IT) 3
Internet Movie Database (IMDb) 115-117

J

journey maps 184-186

K

key performance indicators (KPIs) 14, 28

L

levels of scale
about 122-125
expectations, levelling 125
LinkedIn
about 112
change 114
consequence 114
cooperation 114
coordination 113
local symmetries
reflective symmetry 145
rotational (radial) symmetry 145
translational symmetry 145

M

maps
about 100
Wayfinding 101
meme 15, 16
mental models 84
metrics
financial performance metrics 198
operational performance metrics 198
user satisfaction metrics 199

journey maps 184-186
personas 181
prototyping 193, 194
selecting 180
usability studies 186, 187
visual design 189
Wireframes 193, 194

U

Usability Professional Association (UPA) 161
usability studies
about 186, 187
reporting 188
RITE usability testing 187, 188
User Experience (UX) approach
about 1, 164, 165
business 166
Enterprise UX 165
UX design
creativity, applying 36-38
creativity space 38, 39
patterns 120
UX maturity map
about 176
awareness stage 176
core stage 177
integrated stage 177
repeatable stage 176
strategic stage 176
UX maturity problem
about 160
misunderstanding 163, 164
process game 161-163

UX, measuring
Google terms 200
metrics, using 198
online measurement tools 200
references 199
UX mindset
final story 20-22
problem solving 18-20
UX professionals
challenges 164
UX trade
tools 179

V

visual design 189

W

Wayfinding
characteristics 101
destination recognition 106
orientation 102
reference 101
route decision 103
route monitoring 104, 105
Waze 72
wholeness
about 119
searching 157
wireframes 193, 194

CPSIA information can be obtained
at www.ICGtesting.com
Printed in the USA
LVHW021028080822
725381LV00004B/52